This book's international comparative character that shows that urban childhood may differ globally but overall shares a decline in the building of children's social capital. This is both a sincere loss for children growing up urban and a loss for cities. The social fabric of cities is only deteriorating when we don't change this negative trend. This book was written with a focus on children's outdoor play and social capital, drawing on the results of joint research by researchers from Japan, Sweden, Finland, Germany, Switzerland, and the United Kingdom.

This is a groundbreaking book that suggests ways to rebuild social capital so that children can play outside and grow. Today, there is a tendency to describe about social capital in terms of IT networks. But contrary, this book is showing its originality advocating that social capital through real place is important for children's growth, and presents theories and concrete methods reflecting research findings.

Although there are differences in culture, systems, and social backgrounds between the West and the East, this book transcends these differences and specifically identifies the common spatial and social conditions that promote children's outdoor play. In the final chapter, applying the pattern language method, and follow the illustrated keyword method to extract 107 patterns and show how to review and improve familiar spaces. This book is a must-read not only for children-related researchers and experts, but also for those in charge of urban planning and local government policies.

Lia Karsten, *University of Amsterdam, the Netherlands/UNIMORE University, Italy*

SOCIAL CAPITAL FOR A CHILD-FRIENDLY CITY

Social Capital for a Child-Friendly City argues for the importance of relationship networks (social capital) in children's growth and socialization, and explores how child-friendly social capital can be cultivated through urban planning and community development. As outdoor play decreases and children spend more time online, Kinoshita and Terada return to John Dewey's proposal that social capital is essential for nurturing the next generation and establish a democratic and sustainable society. The book features examples from Sweden, Finland, Germany, Switzerland, the UK, and Japan, exploring methods for cultivating social capital and spaces for children to play and develop in cooperative housing, outdoor play spaces, streets, parks, and neighbourhoods. We express our gratitude to Dr. Marketta Kytta, Professor of Aalto University, who gave valuable suggestions about the key term 'bullerby' and 'social capital'.

This book will be of use to students and practitioners of urban planning and landscape architecture, as well as any community leaders or developers seeking to foster a nurturing environment where children can flourish.

Isami Kinoshita is a Professor at Otsuma Women's University and Professor Emeritus at Chiba University.

Mitsunari Terada (Charlie) is a landscape planner and researcher, and is an Assistant Professor at Nippon Sport Science University.

SOCIAL CAPITAL FOR A CHILD-FRIENDLY CITY

Housing, Streets, and Parks

Edited by Isami Kinoshita and Mitsunari Terada

LONDON AND NEW YORK

Designed cover by Isami Kinoshita and Mitsunari Terada.
Cover photo: Lizzie Coombes
Special thanks: Adrian Sinclair

First published 2025
by Routledge
4 Park Square, Milton Park, Abingdon, Oxon, OX14 4RN

and by Routledge
605 Third Avenue, New York, NY 10158

Routledge is an imprint of the Taylor & Francis Group, an informa business

© 2025 selection and editorial matter, Isami Kinoshita and Mitsunari Terada; individual chapters, the contributors

The right of Isami Kinoshita and Mitsunari Terada to be identified as the authors of the editorial material, and of the authors for their individual chapters, has been asserted in accordance with sections 77 and 78 of the Copyright, Designs and Patents Act 1988.

All rights reserved. No part of this book may be reprinted or reproduced or utilised in any form or by any electronic, mechanical, or other means, now known or hereafter invented, including photocopying and recording, or in any information storage or retrieval system, without permission in writing from the publishers.

Trademark notice: Product or corporate names may be trademarks or registered trademarks, and are used only for identification and explanation without intent to infringe.

British Library Cataloguing-in-Publication Data
A catalogue record for this book is available from the British Library

Library of Congress Cataloging-in-Publication Data
Names: Kinoshita, Isami, editor. | Terada, Mitsunari, editor.
Title: Social capital for a child friendly city : housing, streets, and parks / edited by Isami Kinoshita and Mitsunari Terada.
Description: Abingdon, Oxon ; New York, NY : Routledge, 2025. | Includes bibliographical references and index.
Identifiers: LCCN 2024028505 (print) | LCCN 2024028506 (ebook) | ISBN 9781032597829 (hardback) | ISBN 9781032597812 (paperback) | ISBN 9781003456223 (ebook)
Subjects: LCSH: City children. | Play environments. | Social capital (Sociology) | Child development. | City planning. | Community development.
Classification: LCC HT206 .S63 2025 (print) | LCC HT206 (ebook) | DDC 305.2309173/2—dc23/eng/20240913
LC record available at https://lccn.loc.gov/2024028505
LC ebook record available at https://lccn.loc.gov/2024028506

ISBN: 978-1-032-59782-9 (hbk)
ISBN: 978-1-032-59781-2 (pbk)
ISBN: 978-1-003-45622-3 (ebk)

DOI: 10.4324/9781003456223

Typeset in Sabon
by Apex CoVantage, LLC

CONTENTS

About the editors ix
List of contributors x

PART I
Introduction: children's outdoor play and social capital **1**

1 Swinging on the virtual playground: children's perspectives on green time and screen time 3
   Mitsunari Terada and Mariia Ermilova

2 Social capital and children's outdoor play 16
   Isami Kinoshita

PART II
Cooperative and collective housing spaces **29**

3 Requirements for community and individual developments in outdoor space design: from Freidorf, Switzerland 31
   Urs Maurer

4 Ackermannbogen in Munich, a modern, child-friendly urban village 55
   Kati Landsiedel

viii Contents

5 Child-rearing social capital in collective housing in Japan 77
   Nobuko Matsumoto

PART III
Play spaces and the Bullerby model 85

6 Children's planned and unplanned places of play and encounter in West Herttoniemi, Helsinki 87
   Veera Moll and Eva Purkarthofer

7 Bullerby and the value of physical environments for social capital: a Swedish example in times of change 102
   Märit Jansson

8 Bullerby children in today's Japan: how they play and who supports them 115
   Mari Yoshinaga

PART IV
Streets, parks, and neighbourhoods 127

9 Children's outdoor play and social capital: insights from one London housing scheme 129
   Tim Gill

10 Sharing the street and town is essential for children's growth: from the perspective of *machi hoiku* ('community-embedded nursery') 146
    Norie Miwa

PART V
Conclusion 159

11 Pattern languages to raise social capital for a child-friendly city 161
    Isami Kinoshita and Mitsunari Terada

Index *190*

ABOUT THE EDITORS

Isami Kinoshita is a professor at Otsuma Women's University and professor emeritus at Chiba University. He studied architecture at Tokyo Institute of Technology, earning a PhD in 1984. He has been leading community design workshops for children involving participatory approaches since 1980. One of his well-known works is three-generational play maps that encouraged intergenerational communication among residents of an area in Tokyo; the maps led people to rethink children's play and urban environmental change. Since 2004, he has been lobbying national and local governments to promote the Child-Friendly City Initiative, and since 2016, he has served as the chairperson of the Japan Committee for UNICEF's Child-Friendly City Development Committee.

Mitsunari Terada (Charlie) facilitates child-friendly communities through his work as a landscape planner and researcher. He received his PhD from Chiba University, Japan, in 2020, and currently serves as an assistant professor at Research Institute for Children's Physical Health, Nippon Sport Science University. To create children-friendly communities with multiple stakeholders, he plays and talks with children and advocates for people from local community to central government levels. He lived in a neighborhood association center for 7 years as co-manager. He is also involved in various organizations, serving on the board of IPA Japan, as a senior researcher at the Information Research Center of Japan Adventure Playground Association, as a committee member for inclusive playgrounds in urban parks at the Ministry of Land, Infrastructure, Transport and Tourism, Japan, and on the third-party evaluation committee of UNICEF's Child Friendly Cities Initiative.

CONTRIBUTORS

Mariia Ermilova is an environmental educator, researcher, and community design practitioner. She has been working as a co-manager of the Iwase Neighborhood Association in Matsudo, Japan, since 2016, cultivating native flowers and herbal gardens in the area. She teaches in the Toyo University Department of Sociology and is currently a postdoctoral researcher at Nippon Sport Science University.

Tim Gill is an independent scholar, writer, and consultant based in London, UK, and a global advocate for children's outdoor play and mobility. He is the author of *Urban Playground: How Child-Friendly Planning and Design Can Save Cities* (RIBA Publications, 2021) and *No Fear: Growing Up in a Risk-Averse Society* (Calouste Bulbenkian Foundation, 2007).

Tim is a UK Design Council Ambassador. His consultancy clients include corporation, public bodies, and NGOs from throughout the UK and around the world, and he has spoken to audiences in over 25 countries across six continents. A former director of the Children's Play Council (now Play England), in 2003 he was seconded to the UK civil service to lead a government review into children's play. Tim is a Churchill Fellow and has studied and advised on child-friendly urban planning in North and South America, the Middle East, and Europe. He holds degrees in philosophy and psychology from Oxford and London Universities and an honorary doctorate in education from Edge Hill University, and he is an honorary patron of the UK Forest School Association.

Tim writes for the mainstream media, trade, and academic publications and appears regularly on radio and television. His website is www.rethinkingchildhood.com.

Contributors   xi

Märit Jansson, Associate Professor and Collaboration specialist at the Swedish University of Agricultural Sciences (SLU), has a master's degree in landscape architecture from 2004 and a PhD in landscape planning from 2009, both received at the Swedish University of Agricultural Sciences. Her work experience includes being a research assistant, lecturer, and senior lecturer, with international stays at Chiba University, Japan, and University of Copenhagen, Denmark. She currently leads the theme group on landscape governance and management at SLU. Her research interests include landscape management, landscape governance, and the development of outdoor environments for various user groups. Much of her research work has involved children and their use of neighbourhoods, school grounds, and playgrounds, and she received the Brio prize in 2016 for one of the books she has co-edited, on Swedish playgrounds. Another of her co-edited books is *Urban Open Space Governance and Management* (Routledge). Through her work as a collaboration specialist, she also contributes to the connections between academia and practice in mainly landscape architecture.

Kati Landsiedel is a psychologist and environmental educator at PA Spielkultur e.V in Munich (NGO Play & Social Work). Kati manages PA/SPIELkultur's nature and sustainability program and has conceptually devised many of the current projects. Kati believes that sustainable, sociable lifestyles happen when people develop good relationships with themselves and their environments and have many opportunities to learn what really makes them happy and satisfied. This learning process should be as playful as possible, appeal to all senses, and be fun. Crucial for these learning processes are healthy, secure, and socially apt environments that give children possibilities to explore and experiment safely and autonomously.

Nobuko Matsumoto is Professor of Social Information Studies at Otsuma Women's University. Matsumoto's expertise is in the fields of housing, urban planning, and community building in built-up areas, and her research to date has clarified the structure of the transformation of living environments by immediately and intelligently analysing the relationship between the renewal of residential urban areas and the life cycles of residents. This research focuses on two types of aging in residential areas that lead to housing problems and deterioration of the living environment and ways to improve the housing issues of residents and the urban environment by connecting the two.

Urs Maurer is an architect and spatial planner, gymnastics and sports teacher, teacher, and adult educator. He has conducted research the historical, pedagogical, and philosophical aspects of school construction; his doctoral research at TU Eindhoven was titled "Thinking, Feeling and Willing the Schoolhouse Anew. A Renewal of Foundations, Paradigms and Perspectives." He was a senior assistant at ETHZ, has spent 20 years as a lecturer and examiner for healthy and sustainable building at the SIB Building Biology Training Centre, and for 15 years has run his own office for school space development, Archi-Lecture & LearnScaping. Maurer is also the head of a school space development department in the engineering company Basler & Hofmann AG.

Norie Miwa is a professor at the Graduate School of Urban Society and Culture, Yokohama City University. After working at a design office, Miwa pursued a career as a university researcher. Her expertise is in construction/urban planning, community building, and environmental psychology, and she has researched the relationship between children of different developmental stages and the community. She has also given lectures on child rearing and community development to government officials, child-rearing supporters, and community development organizations.

Veera Moll holds a master's degree in social sciences with a specialization in economic and social history from the University of Helsinki, Finland. Currently, she works as a doctoral researcher at Aalto University, Department of Built Environment in Espoo, Finland. Her forthcoming thesis focuses on children's role in post-war urban planning in Helsinki, Finland. Veera has authored several articles on the urban history of children, exploring it both from a planning perspective and through the lens of children's experiences. In addition to children's urban history, her research interests encompass child-friendly urban planning, playgrounds, standardization of children's play environments, and children's changing mobility in urban contexts.

Eva Purkarthofer holds a master's degree in spatial planning from Vienna University of Technology, Austria, and a PhD from Aalto University, Finland. She currently works as a post-doctoral researcher in the Department of Built Environment, Aalto University. She has been a visiting professor at the University of Vienna and a visiting researcher at San Diego State University, USA, and TU Delft, the Netherlands. Her research interests include European spatial development and EU cohesion policy, strategic urban and regional planning, planning cultures, and planning systems as well as the roles of actors and institutions in planning. She is the coordinator of the AESOP thematic group Transboundary Planning and Governance and an editor at *European Journal of Spatial Development*. She has published in numerous international journals and recently authored the book *Spatial Planning and the European Union. Europeanisation from Within* (Routledge, 2024).

Mari Yoshinaga has conducted research and practice on children's play and mental/physical development from a community psychology perspective and on the nature of child-friendly communities. The 4th generation play map in Setagaya, Tokyo has made by the team Asobi to Machi including Dr. Isami Kinoshita, an editor of this book and me as a member, is the supreme tool for elucidate the poor environment of children's play processing in modern urban area like other big city in world wide. She is a nationally certified clinical psychologist and child care worker and is also involved in the developing a system to rescue the SOS of children in difficult situations. She is a professor at Showa Pharmaceutical University, where she also works as a counsellor for students' mental health.

PART I
Introduction
Children's outdoor play and social capital

1

SWINGING ON THE VIRTUAL PLAYGROUND

Children's perspectives on green time and screen time

Mitsunari Terada and Mariia Ermilova

1. Introduction

Video game as outdoor play

Today, many children spend more time on devices than on playing outdoors, despite the presumably adverse impacts on health and development. In this chapter, we examine the state of children's play activities globally, with particular focus on the recent increase in screen time, and explore potential solutions to maintain enriching 'green time' in a new reality. Drawing on survey findings, we discuss trends in children's play activities in both urban and rural contexts.

The photo in Figure 1.1, taken at a neighbourhood park in Japan, shows two children playing video games on a stationary swing. A younger sibling sits nearby, awaiting his turn with the coveted device. This prompts two key questions:

1. Is this truly outdoor play? Have you observed similar scenes in your country?
2. Is this playground engaging and inviting? What does a typical playground look like in your country?

To address the first question, the definitions must be clarified. While the children are physically outside, this activity seems distinct from the often idealised, imaginative, social outdoor play. As some local children explained in interviews, this allows them to play video games without parental time limits while also engaging in other activities when they grow bored with the games.

DOI: 10.4324/9781003456223-2

FIGURE 1.1   Children playing video games on swings in a park.

Regarding the second question, the space is hardly an attractive playground: a deserted area enclosed by a fence. It is, therefore, not surprising that children are not eager or excited to play there. The virtual world on a screen can stimulate curiosity far more than this outdoor space. How inviting and engaging are the play spaces in our local areas? Can they provide rich, varied experiences for children?

Playing is both enjoyable and a fundamental right for all children, apart from being critical for cognitive, physical, social, and emotional development. Despite its importance, enshrined in Article 31 of the UN Convention on the Rights of the Child, play is 'the forgotten right' in society (UN Committee on the Rights of the Child, 2013). As daily life evolves rapidly, the nature and perception of children's outdoor play are also changing. Consequently, we must amplify children's voices in this discussion: Why are local play areas not updated like our games? How can we update them?

Definitions

This chapter focuses on children's free time, excluding adult-organised activities in schools, clubs, and other structured pursuits. In this chapter, we define screen time as time spent interacting with screens, including playing games, using social media, and watching TV. Additionally, we use the umbrella term green time to encompass all outdoor play activities. As discussed in the case of Figure 1.1, we acknowledge that green time does not necessarily involve direct contact with vegetation and may even include outdoor video games. While controversial, this hybrid play still provides children with the required melatonin for healthy sleep patterns (Noi & Shikano, 2011).

The term green time appears frequently in research on health, especially mental health (Langley, 2021; Oswald et al., 2020). For instance, it is a potential treatment for ADHD (Faber Taylor & Kuo, 2011). Some define green time narrowly, as 'young people's contact with nature' (Oswald et al., 2020). However, most researchers avoid quantifying children's natural interactions solely by the time they spend outside. Instead, they use terms like 'affordances' to assess the accessibility and explore the meaning of green spaces, foliage, trees, and greenery near homes (Laaksoharju & Rappe, 2017) or evaluate the use of nature spaces, placing them on a "nature continuum" (Gundersen et al., 2016). Others examine specific nature experiences, like touching plants and insects, negatively framing the lack of these as an 'extinction of experience' (Soga & Gaston, 2016). In our broad definition, the term green time encompasses outdoor play, nature experiences, and related activities and is not limited to any one category.

2. Method

In this chapter, we frequently invoke the voices of children, which we derived from our own research data. We conducted ethnographic fieldwork while residing in a neighbourhood association building in an urban area of Japan over a period of seven years beginning in March 2016. We also conducted interviews while overseeing the planning of two rural playgrounds from 2015 to 2020. Overall, this work comprises interviews with children aged six to 15 years. Additionally, we draw on a questionnaire from our prior research while discussing children's play activities in Japanese urban and rural locales (Terada et al. 2020). These questionnaires, administered with cooperation from municipal schools, gathered data on play time, space, friends, activities, and more.

3. Green time and screen time in children's play

Green time and why we have less of it

The following quote from an eight-year-old boy in rural Japan encapsulates the richness and variability of outdoor play:

> It is fun to play outside because you never get bored. We start playing football, then it changes to tag, then catching bugs, and the play transforms based on who's there, so it never gets boring. Video games are fun too, but

they're the same over and over. Here (in this mountain area) we change games by season, and we forget what we did last year, so it feels new to us, which is fun!

Fortunately, this boy has playmates living nearby, a rarity in rural Japan, where children sometimes reside long distances apart and commute to consolidated schools by bus (Terada et al., 2020). His description of seasonal play exemplifies the increasingly uncommon but valuable green time. This enriching play depends on independent mobility within a community and environmental affordances, encapsulated in the Bullerby model (Kyttä, 2003).

Outdoor play provides critical cognitive, social, emotional, and physical benefits for child development (Woolley et al., 2009). For example, Woolley and coauthors (2009) groups the advantages of nature play into three broad categories: 1) cognitive and social development, 2) physical and mental health and well-being, and 3) how childhood experiences shape adult values, behaviours, and actions. Green time is foundational for healthy growth. First – and foremost – outdoor environments provide opportunities for social interaction with peers and adults. Experts suggest that the mixed-age social groups that often spontaneously form during outdoor play allow younger children to learn from older role models, while older children can practise leadership skills (Gray, 2011). Additionally, exposure to green spaces confers individual cognitive and mental benefits including improved cognitive functioning (Wells, 2000); increased self-esteem, personal autonomy, self-concept, and interpersonal abilities (Kellert & Derr, 1998); and greater self-confidence, self-awareness, and resilience (Kaplan & Talbot, 1983). A survey in Japan revealed that adults who were more enthusiastic players in childhood tended to possess higher self-esteem and resilience (Japanese Ministry of Education, Culture, Sports, Science and Technology, 2017).

Second, green time provides extensive health benefits, including improved mental (Tillmann et al., 2018; Oswald et al., 2020) and physical (Mygind et al., 2019) health. Third, significant childhood experiences in nature make adults more likely to engage in environmental stewardship (Chawla, 2007). However, research identifies interrelated factors creating barriers to green time for today's children. Key obstacles include reduced discretionary time due to packed school and extracurricular schedules (Ginsburg et al., 2007); screen time – television and digital media (Clements, 2004), parental fears about injury, traffic, and strangers (Valentine & McKendrck, 1997; Johansson, 2006); diminished access to natural areas and biodiversity in increasingly urbanised settings (Soga et al., 2018); and declining independent mobility (Shaw et al., 2013; Kyttä et al., 2015).

Green time is declining in Japan as well. A survey conducted on nearly 4,000 schoolchildren aged 6–12 years, in 2020–2021, revealed that 30%–50% do not play outside on weekdays after school (Figure 1.2); percentages

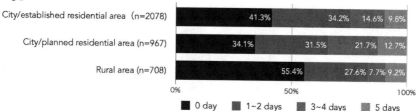
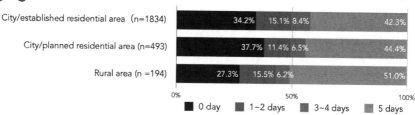

FIGURE 1.2 Numbers of days: outdoor play (green time) and screen time on weekdays.

were especially high in rural areas (50%–60%) (Kinoshita & Terada, 2023). Rural children also spent more screen time (1+ hours daily) after school. Declining birth rates and school consolidation may have reduced neighbourhood playmates and limited recognition of nature as play space. About 40%–50% of children across all regions engage in daily screen time on weekdays, substituting it for outdoor play, a pattern mirrored elsewhere (e.g. Larson et al., 2019; Loebach et al., 2021).

Screen time: video games as outdoor play

To illustrate the dynamic shift from green to screen time, we refer again to children's voices, citing an interview with an 11-year-old boy from the neighbourhood. We were in contact with him for seven years (2016–2023). He is creative and enjoys playing outside, but shared thoughts on mixing outdoor play with video games:

> I did not expect video games to count as outdoor play. I wanted to play tag, ball games, etc. But some friends kept playing Nintendo Switch and others joined in. Suddenly I felt alone and stopped going to the playground for a year.

He used to play with friends at a nearby park, but they often brought video games. Though they did play tag when tired of screens, the activities predominantly depended on the group's mood that day. His mother voiced concerns about his struggle:

> It is difficult to make friends without the same video game, so I told him to buy the one they have.

Gradually, peer pressure triumphed, as the boy explained:

> After a year, I bought the same video game as my friends and joined playing video games. Now I am glad to be in the cycle. I totally depend on the game when I do not have club activity.

We asked what cycle he meant, and he explained (Figure 1.3):

> We are caught in a cycle of playing video games and watching YouTube. When we get stuck or want to enjoy the game more, YouTubers teach us how. When we get bored with one game, we just switch games and do the same thing. But to talk to friends, I need to play the same game as them.

During the year before the interview, he was noticed playing video games extensively. Even three years after the interview, the boy reported remaining in this loop of on-screen play (Tomita et al., 2020). Despite his initial apprehensions, he has now developed a taste for video games and feels satisfied.

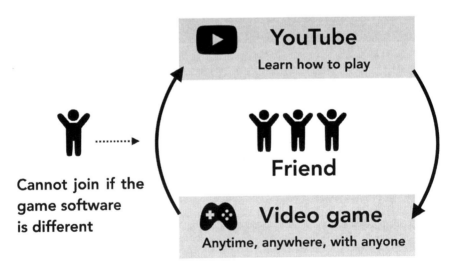

FIGURE 1.3 Cycle of screen-based play.

Negative and positive aspects of screen time

Excessive screen use has become a global issue, with the WHO classifying it as an addiction disorder. Specialists raise concerns about the negative impacts of screen time on children. For example, studies confirm that screen time acts as a risk, while green time is a protective factor for children's mental health (Oswald et al., 2020; Camerini et al., 2022). Regarding children's screen activities, social media, online games, and videos may increase depressive tendencies (Kidokoro et al., 2022). Greater screen time is also associated with reduced mental imagery among children (Suggate & Martzog, 2020). Research on toddlers indicates that screen time displaces peer play, potentially offsetting negative links between screens and development (Putnick et al., 2023).

However, some take an optimistic view of video games that connect children to nature. Games have 'expanded from domestic to public space', merging real and virtual worlds and sometimes simulating nature (Chang, 2019). As Christine Paulsen and Jessica Andrews report, technology can, surprisingly, motivate families to explore nature (Paulsen & Andrews, 2019). Video games can also facilitate child participation in designing play spaces; for example Block-by-Block studio using Minecraft for "playful public participation" (Delaney, 2022).

Pokémon, originating in Japan, is a prime example of video games mimicking nature. The game became globally popular and spurred research on its role in the relationship between children and nature. Some argue that the narrative of creating Pokémon to connect urban children to nature reflects limited access to nature (Santry, 2019). Pokémon's story world interweaves environmentalism, biodiversity, and materialism (Bainbridge, 2014), teaching ecological interactions (Rangel et al. 2022). Playing Pokémon GO increases physical activity (Liang et al., 2023). Games also provide socialisation, which is vital in rural Japan, where children live far apart from each other. Interviews revealed that rural children use wi-fi to interact with school friends and play together online (Terada, 2020), supplementing in-person play, as confirmed elsewhere (Ferguson & Olson, 2013).

Let us illustrate the fusion of video games and real play (Figure 1.4) from our participatory observation in the local community. Children became excited about working tools like shovels, rakes, especially a pickaxe, which reminded them of the game Minecraft. They happily excavated items like broken glass, pottery, and garbage from the soil while we conversed with them as playleaders. From this observation, we conclude that with encouragement from a playleader, children can apply the knowledge gained from video games to play creatively with natural elements. In other words, knowledge about the natural environment from video games can be applied to play situations in the real world given appropriate affordances.

FIGURE 1.4   Excavation pickaxe play in a neighbourhood park, inspired by the video game Minecraft.

Through years of interacting with neighbourhood children, we have found that they actually dig soil and build secret bases more in Minecraft than in reality. They run and dance more in Fortnite than in reality. They fish and explore forests more in Animal Crossing than in reality. They hunt Pokémon more than insects. As a first step to supporting outdoor play, we must acknowledge these realities and leverage games to prompt outdoor play.

4. Conclusion: encourage green time

Updating outdoor play spaces?

Children today spend more time interacting with screens than engaging in outdoor play. As illustrated throughout this chapter, while excessive screen time presents risks, certain games also offer benefits by motivating outdoor play, teaching about nature, and providing remote socialisation. Ultimately, as our research reveals, children feel caught in a self-reinforcing cycle of video games and online videos. Specifically, rural youth face social isolation and depend on virtual play. Although some games promote outdoor exploration, most still displace physical and social activities that are vital for development.

During our interviews, a 12-year-old boy from an urban area asked us the following: "Games are constantly updating any bugs. But why have the playgrounds in the parks never been updated?" He observed that in virtual spaces, players experience regular updates, such as new stages, events, and items, as well as fixes for bugs. In contrast, playground equipment does not change or evolve, and prohibitions on play freedom are not readily updated. Indeed, as he points out, programmers are continually organising new game stages and events to engage children's attention, but there is no variation or upgrading in playground equipment. In Japan, the standard set of play equipment in a park consists of a sandbox, slide, and swing; in many parks, the same set was installed for decades. This approach of installing one set of equipment was named Kit, Fence, Carpet approach and was criticised as being unattractive to children (Woolley & Lowe, 2013).

The concept of 'update' is emblematic of industrial society, criticised by philosopher Ivan Illich (1973). Illich argued that tools (including physical objects like smartphone and social systems like school) can evolve from being convivial to manipulative, constraining freedom, and autonomy. Change is visible in the shift from values to institutions (institutionalization), from verb to noun. For example, the verb 'playing' became unified into static entities like playgrounds, play equipment, and video games in the minds of children and adults.

Play can happen anywhere: on the street, in the field or forest. However, children we talked to in rural Japan are often demanding new playgrounds and struggling to play elsewhere.

Restoring the play ecosystem through tools

Illich posits that to mitigate potential adverse effects, it is crucial to moderate the nature of 'tools' rather than human consciousness. This raises the question: how should we position 'tools' within the context of play?

Firstly, the realm of 'institutionalized/planned' play spaces commonly provided for children, such as playgrounds and parks, should be continually reinvented, just as video games iteratively evolve to engage users. The use of natural elements is widely suggested as a solution to the issue of boring playgrounds (Woolley & Lowe, 2013). A radical suggestion is to enrich parks with landscape elements for play, which will render play equipment unnecessary (Woolley, 2008). Another example of a place for children that is 'reinvented' and 'updated' is an adventure playground. Environments can be enhanced with loose parts that children can manipulate and update.

Secondly, we must broaden our conceptualization of 'play spaces' beyond merely institutionalized areas like parks and playgrounds. Instead, we should envision the entire community as a potential playground, encompassing residential streets, vacant lots, groves, forests, and waterways. Based on children's perspectives, researchers highlight the value of 'unmanaged', 'unprogrammed' nature play spaces (Jansson et al., 2016) where children's fantasies and desires for outdoor play are fulfilled (Wales et al., 2021). Just as the virtual world is infinitely mutable, green play spaces represent ultimate impermanence, evolution, and experimentation.

Thirdly, to catalyse the relationship between children and these diverse play environments mentioned above, it is advisable to deploy professionals such as play workers or local coordinators. Just as content creators on digital platforms like YouTube serve as play facilitators in the virtual realm, it could be helpful to have analogous facilitators for outdoor play experiences. With the earlier excavation example, on receiving support like tools and place, the children tapped into the affordances of the land to dig, build, role play, and explore. An invested playleader can extract the play potential in outdoor spaces through prompting, modelling playful curiosity, and encouraging child-driven adventures that arise organically from the surroundings. Rather than passive supervision, playleader adults perform an active role in building those environments and nurturing the child–environment interplay that is the heart of green time. Investing in playleaders, whether parents, educators, or community members, can unlock rich play ecologies even in relatively mundane natural spaces.

To effectively implement this framework, it is essential to foster a holistic play ecosystem within communities that encompasses both physical infrastructure and human capital. A critical step is the identification and development of play opportunities that can be seamlessly woven into diverse local settings, utilising available community resources. The erosion of play spaces occurred gradually over the past century, and the process of regenerating a vibrant play ecosystem may require a similarly extended timeframe. This long-term restoration effort necessitates the revitalization of each space's playability through collaborative engagement with various local stakeholders, reflecting a multi-generational commitment to enriching children's play environments.

Grant information

This work was supported by JSPS KAKENHI Grant Number JP20H02323, and JP22K14912.

References

Bainbridge, J. (2014). 'It is a Pokémon world': The Pokémon franchise and the environment. *International Journal of Cultural Studies*, 17(4), 399–414.

Camerini, A. L., Albanese, E., Marciano, L., & Corona Immunitas Research Group. (2022). The impact of screen time and green time on mental health in children and adolescents during the COVID-19 pandemic. *Computers in Human Behavior Reports*, 7, 100204.

Chaarani, B., Ortigara, J., Yuan, D., Loso, H., Potter, A., & Garavan, H. P. (2022). Association of video gaming with cognitive performance among children. *JAMA Network Open, 5*(10), e2235721.

Chang, A. Y. (2019). *Playing nature: Ecology in video games (Vol. 58)*. University of Minnesota Press.

Chawla, L. (2007). Childhood experiences associated with care for the natural world: A theoretical framework for empirical results. *Children, Youth and Environments, 17*(4), 144–170.

Clements, R. (2004). An investigation of the status of outdoor play. *Contemporary Issues in Early Childhood, 5*(1), 68–80.

Delaney, J. (2022). Minecraft and playful public participation in Urban design. *Urban Planning, 7*(2), 330–342.

Faber Taylor, A., & Kuo, F. E. (2011). Could exposure to everyday green spaces help treat ADHD? Evidence from children's play settings. *Applied Psychology: Health and Well-Being, 3*(3), 281–303.

Ferguson, C. J., & Olson, C. K. (2013). Friends, fun, frustration and fantasy: Child motivations for video game play. *Motivation and Emotion, 37*, 154–164.

Ginsburg, K. R., American Academy of Pediatrics Committee on Communications, & American Academy of Pediatrics Committee on Psychosocial Aspects of Child and Family Health. (2007). The importance of play in promoting healthy child development and maintaining strong parent-child bonds. *Pediatrics, 119*(1), 182–191.

Gray, P. (2011). The special value of children's age-mixed play. *American Journal of Play, 3*(4), 500–522.

Gundersen, V., Skår, M., O'Brien, L., Wold, L. C., & Follo, G. (2016). Children and nearby nature: A nationwide parental survey from Norway. *Urban Forestry & Urban Greening, 17*, 116–125.

Illich, I. (1973). *Tools for conviviality*. Marion Boyars.

Jansson, M., Sundevall, E., & Wales, M. (2016). The role of green spaces and their management in a child-friendly urban village. *Urban Forestry & Urban Greening, 18*, 228–236.

Japanese Ministry of Education, Culture, Sports, Science and Technology. (2017). *Reiwa ni nendo seisyounen no taikenkatsudo ni kansuru chousakenkyukettukahoukoku (Report on the results of research into youth experience activities in 2020)*. Retrieved February 26, 2023, from https://www.mext.go.jp/content/20210908-mxt_chisui01-100003338_2.pdf

Johansson, M. (2006). Environment and parental factors as determinants of mode for children's leisure travel. *Journal of Environmental Psychology, 26*(2), 156–169.

Kaplan, S., & Talbot, J. F. (1983). Psychological benefits of a wilderness experience. In *Behavior and the natural environment* (pp. 163–203). Springer US.

Kellert, S. R., & Derr, V. (1998). *A national study of outdoor wilderness experience* (ERIC Document Reproduction Service No. ED444748). Yale University, School of Forestry and Environmental Studies.

Kidokoro, T., Shikano, A., Tanaka, R., Tanabe, K., Imai, N., & Noi, S. (2022). Different types of screen behavior and depression in children and adolescents. *Frontiers in Pediatrics, 9*, 822603.

Kinoshita, I., & Terada, M. (2023). *Kodomo machizukuri catalogue (Children's community design catalogue)*. Kajima Institute Publishing.

Kyttä, M. (2003). *Children in outdoor contexts: Affordances and independent mobility in the assessment of environmental child friendliness*. Helsinki University of Technology.

Kyttä, M., Hirvonen, J., Rudner, J., Pirjola, I., & Laatikainen, T. (2015). The last free-range children? Children's independent mobility in Finland in the 1990s and 2010s. *Journal of Transport Geography, 47*, 1–12.

Laaksoharju, T., & Rappe, E. (2017). Trees as affordances for connectedness to place – A framework to facilitate children's relationship with nature. *Urban Forestry & Urban Greening, 28,* 150–159.

Langley, J. L. (2021). Nature play therapy and telemental health: How green time and screen time play well together. In *Play therapy and telemental health* (pp. 217–228). Routledge.

Larson, L. R., Szczytko, R., Bowers, E. P., Stephens, L. E., Stevenson, K. T., & Floyd, M. F. (2019). Outdoor time, screen time, and connection to nature: Troubling trends among rural youth?. *Environment and Behavior, 51*(8), 966–991.

Liang, H., Wang, X., & An, R. (2023). Influence of Pokémon GO on physical activity and psychosocial well-being in children and adolescents: Systematic review. *Journal of Medical Internet Research, 25,* e49019.

Loebach, J., Sanches, M., Jaffe, J., & Elton-Marshall, T. (2021). Paving the way for outdoor play: Examining socio-environmental barriers to community-based outdoor play. *International Journal of Environmental Research and Public Health, 18*(7), 3617.

Mygind, L., Kjeldsted, E., Hartmeyer, R., Mygind, E., Bølling, M., & Bentsen, P. (2019). Mental, physical and social health benefits of immersive nature-experience for children and adolescents: A systematic review and quality assessment of the evidence. *Health & Place, 58,* 102136.

Noi, S., & Shikano, A. (2011). Melatonin metabolism and living conditions among children on weekdays and holidays, and living factors related to melatonin metabolism. *School Health, 7,* 25–34.

Oswald, T. K., Rumbold, A. R., Kedzior, S. G., & Moore, V. M. (2020). Psychological impacts of "screen time" and "green time" for children and adolescents: A systematic scoping review. *PLoS One, 15*(9), e0237725.

Paulsen, C. A., & Andrews, J. R. (2019). Using screen time to promote green time: Outdoor STEM education in OST settings. *Afterschool Matters, 30,* 24–32.

Putnick, D. L., Trinh, M. H., Sundaram, R., Bell, E. M., Ghassabian, A., Robinson, S. L., & Yeung, E. (2023). Displacement of peer play by screen time: Associations with toddler development. *Pediatric Research, 93*(5), 1425–1431.

Rangel, D. F., Lima, J. S., Da Silva, E. F. N., Ferreira, K. D. A., & Costa, L. L. (2022). Pokémon as a playful and didactic tool for teaching about ecological interactions. *Journal of Biological Education,* 1–11.

Santry, E. (2019). Pokémon and the environment. In *The augmented reality of Pokémon GO: Chronotopes, moral panic, and other complexities* (p. 17). Lexington Books.

Shaw, B., Watson, B., Frauendienst, B., Redecker, A., Jones, T., & Hillman, M. (2013). *Children's independent mobility: A comparative study in England and Germany (1971-2010).* Policy Studies Institute.

Soga, M., & Gaston, K. J. (2016). Extinction of experience: The loss of human–nature interactions. *Frontiers in Ecology and the Environment, 14*(2), 94–101.

Soga, M., Yamanoi, T., Tsuchiya, K., Koyanagi, T. F., & Kanai, T. (2018). What are the drivers of and barriers to children's direct experiences of nature?. *Landscape and Urban Planning, 180,* 114–120.

Suggate, S. P., & Martzog, P. (2020). Screen-time influences children's mental imagery performance. *Developmental Science, 23*(6), e12978.

Terada, M. (2020). *Kodomo no sotoasobi no chiiki gabanansu: Risuku shakai wo norikoerutame ni* [Local governance for children's outdoor play: Growing beyond risk]. Doctoral dissertation, Chiba University.

Terada, M., Ermilova, M., & Kinoshita, I. (2020). Study on the current situation of children's play through a comparison of three generations in a rural area-case of Ishikawa Town, Fukushima Prefecture. *Transactions of AIJ. Journal of Architecture, Planning and Environmental Engineering, 85*(768), 307–316.

Tillmann, S., Tobin, D., Avison, W., & Gilliland, J. (2018). Mental health benefits of interactions with nature in children and teenagers: A systematic review. *Journal of Epidemiology and Community Health, 72*(10), 958–966.

Tomita, Y., Terada, M., Ermilova, M., Kinoshita, I. (2020). Soto asobimo game ni boku ga kouen ni modorenakunatta wake (Playing outside is also a 'game' – why I can't go back to the park anymore . . .). *Child, Youth and Environmental Studies, 17*(1), 55.

UN Committee on the Rights of the Child (CRC). (2013, April 17). *General comment No. 17 (2013) on the right of the child to rest, leisure, play, recreational activities, cultural life and the arts (art. 31)*, CRC/C/GC/17.

Valentine, G., & McKendrck, J. (1997). Children's outdoor play: Exploring parental concerns about children's safety and the changing nature of childhood. *Geoforum, 28*(2), 219–235.

Wales, M., Mårtensson, F., & Jansson, M. (2021). 'You can be outside a lot': Independent mobility and agency among children in a suburban community in Sweden. *Children's Geographies, 19*(2), 184–196.

Wells, N. M. (2000). At home with nature: Effects of "greenness" on children's cognitive functioning. *Environment and Behavior, 32*(6), 775–795.

Woolley, H. (2008). Watch this space! Designing for children's play in public open spaces. *Geography Compass, 2*(2), 495–512. ISSN 1749-8198.

Woolley, H., & Lowe, A. (2013). Exploring the relationship between design approach and play value of outdoor play spaces. *Landscape Research, 38*(1), 53–74.

Woolley, H., Pattacini, L., & Somerset-ward, A. (2009). *Children and the natural environment: Experiences, influences and interventions – summary*. Natural England research reports (Number 040). Natural England.

2
SOCIAL CAPITAL AND CHILDREN'S OUTDOOR PLAY

Isami Kinoshita

1. Introduction

The world is currently facing multiple crises: the climate crisis due to global warming, unprecedented pandemics like COVID-19, and frequent natural disasters, as well as crises of world peace and democracy. Children are always the biggest victims of the personal political interests of those in power, as seen in Russia's invasion of Ukraine, Israel's invasion of Gaza, and other military conflicts. These hinder hope for the future and represent major crises for sustainability. The surest way to deal with these crises corresponds to the slogan 'think globally, act locally', which has already spread in the wake of 'Only One Earth' (Dubos & Ward, 1972) at the UN Conference on the Human Environment. It is a bottom-up approach to a sustainable society from the local community.

Turning our attention to our familiar regions and communities, we now live in a world of convenience where people can shop, learn new information, and experience entertainment such as music and movies online without leaving the house; this has been made possible by the rapid progress in IT. The development of this advanced information consumption society will affect children, and the influence will soon appear. Similar to a canary, it foretells the negative side.

We have grasped the reality of children's outdoor play in the past several years. A survey of all grades of elementary school revealed that approximately 80% of children in large cities, 70% in regional cities, and 60% in rural areas do not play outside on weekdays (Figure 2.1). The indoorisation (the increased indoor living) of life means weakening communication and human relations in the neighbourhood. Considering this, how can we rebuild social capital today?

DOI: 10.4324/9781003456223-3

Social capital and children's outdoor play 17

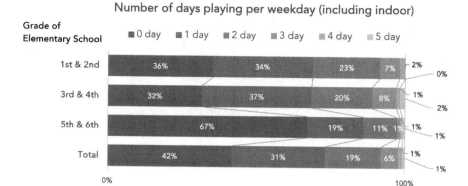

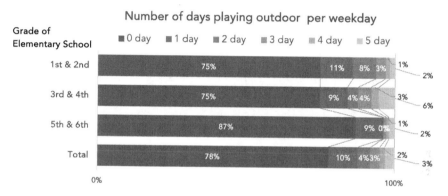

FIGURE 2.1 Number of children's playing days per week and weekday, Chiba City, 2017.

2. Declining birth rates because of social isolation

How can we form a sustainable society by cutting off contact with our neighbours and only interacting with people and things we like online? This indicates the isolation of life. Parenting, especially for the first time, can be lonely, and can lead to mental or emotional ill health. At home, we often see isolated parents who do not express their difficulties and do not receive the necessary support is not available. Young people's anxiety about raising children and concerns about the future of society are accelerating the trend of declining birth rates.

3. Social capital that raises children

By forming groups, human beings have built safe and nurturing societies; people feel safe when they are close to each other, and they survive by helping each other. Liveable space establishes the principles of human society

(Dubos, 1968). The invisible web of human relationships has a function known as social capital.

Social capital refers to the invisible meshes that support the life of a community; if these connections were converted into money and outsourced, the expense would be considerable, and converting them into public services would increase the tax burden. Here, we stress that we are *not* proposing monetising social capital to cut costs; this is because many of the functions of social capital cannot be converted into money. In particular, the role of the social environment in supporting children to play safely outdoors with friends, interact with adults in the community, and grow into members of society cannot be standardised because there are many variations depending on place and cultural background. However, the importance of social capital that supports the growth of children is universal, as evidenced by the common African proverb that "it takes a village to raise a child", and similar ideas can be seen all over the world. This is instinctive and common to the animal world as well; it is a basic function related to the preservation of species embedded in the genes of the DNA as a kind of reciprocal support system.

4. When social capital attracted attention

The term 'social capital' became popular in Japan when the NPO Law was enacted and the expectations for NPOs (non-profit organisations) rose. The Cabinet Office entrusted the investigation to a private research institute (the Japan Research Institute). This report was made public, and it is introduced as follows:

> 'Social Capital' (hereafter referred to as SC) is a characteristic of social organisations such as 'trust', 'norms', and 'networks', and it is said to lead cooperative actions toward a common goal. In other words, it can be understood as social ties or rich human relationships backed by trust.
> *(Cabinet Office, Government of Japan, 2003)*

The concept is based on Robert D Putnam's book *Bowling Alone* (Putnam, 2000). However, Putnam's ideal democracy was the civic structure of tradition and reform of the community in northern Italy (Putnam et al., 1992). He analyses the consequences and outcomes of the reform in the local government system in Italy and examines the conditions under which democracy works well. He found that it depends on social capital, such as mutual trust and social cooperation, in a community with strong traditional elements.

Putnam expressed the following: 'the first known use of the concept was not by cloistered theoretician, but by a practical reformer of the Progressive Era L.J. Hanifan, state supervisor of rural school in West Virginia' (Putnam et al., 1992).

Hanifan invoked the idea of social capital while arguing for the importance of community involvement in successful schools:

> Those tangible substances [that] count for most in the daily lives of people: namely good will, fellowship, sympathy, and social intercourse among the individuals and families who make up social unit. . . . The individual is helpless socially, if left to himself. . . . If he comes into contact with his neighbor, and they twitch other neighbors, there will be an accumulation of social capital, which may immediately satisfy his social needs and which may bear a social potentiality sufficient to the substantial improvement of living conditions in the whole community.
>
> *(Putnam, 2000, p. 19)*

He explains the transformation of the concept of social capital in the following words:

> In the 1960s, by urbanist Jane Jacobs to laud neighborliness in the modern metropolis, in the 1970s by the economist Glenn Loury to analyze the social legacy of slavery, and the 1980s by French social theorist Pierre Bourdieu and by German economist Ekkehart Schlicht to underline the social and economic resources embodied in social networks. Sociologist James S. Coleman put the term firmly and finally on the intellectual agenda in the late 1980s, using it (as Hanifan had originally done) to highlight the social context of education.
>
> *(Putnam, 2000, p. 19)*

5. Traditional and modern concepts

Here, we consider an oversight into Putnam's short-circuiting of the concept of education. The term 'social capital' was first used by John Dewey in 1899 in his book *The School and Society*, and it was later developed by Hanifan. Social capital cannot be converted into money in functions such as education, safety, welfare (mutual aid), health, hygiene, entertainment, and purpose in life. Dewey and Hanifan also show that school functions to form future human capital in the form of children. However, education is not limited to schools. I believe that Dewey and Hanifan argued for community as a place to accumulate capital for human development, which cannot be achieved by schools alone. This can be seen in the following description by Jane Jacobs:

> In real life, only from the ordinary adults of the city sidewalks do children learn – if they learn it at all – the first fundamental of successful city life: People must take a modicum of public responsibility for each other even if they have no ties to each other. Its first principle is that people, even if they have no connection with each other, must have some public

responsibility to each other. This is a lesson nobody learns by being told. It is learned from the experience of having *other people without ties of kinship or close friendship or formal responsibility to you* take a modicum of public responsibility for you.

(Jacobs, 1961, p. 82)

Similarly, Colin Ward used vivid photographs of children playing on the streets and interacting with society through various experiences (Ward, 1978). Introducing this idea as Happy Habitat, he proposed and put into practice how streets can be used as a place for children to play and learn, so as not to end up simply being nostalgic (Ward & Fyson, 1973). He re-introduced the concept as Happy Habitat Revisited. Rather than simply reminiscing about the good old days, he proposed and put into practice streets as places for children to play and learn. He called the streets "exploding schools", outdoor rather than in indoor classrooms, and he considered the concept an attempt to restore both the educational and social capital functions of raising the children of communities that had been lost due to the systemisation of schools, which Dewey saw as problematic.

According to Bourdieu, place-based human relationships, such as the socialisation of children on the streets, came to be understood as social networks regardless of location. It started when he defined human capital (or social resources and values in general) as cultural, economic, and social capital (Bourdieu, 1977). Expanded on by Coleman, this became the concepts of trust, human relationships, and intermediate groups for the human capital of the individual. However, it is clear from the explanations by Dewey (1899) and Jacobs (1961) that the original concept was not limited to human relationships (Table 2.1).

Here, I think we should consider social capital as an environment that includes places (niches). How does it contribute to the growth of next-generation human resources in the sense of invisible (non-money) capital?

6. A liveable space: a space for building social relationships

We consider Dewey's, Hanifan's, and Jacobs' concepts of social capital as place based and traditional, in contrast with the contemporary social capital

TABLE 2.1 Comparing traditional and modern social capital.

	Trust	Potlatch	Human right	Child growth	Place based	Neighbour relationship	Broad Network
Traditional SC	O	O	O	O	O	O	×
Modern SC	O	△	O	△	×	△	O

of Bourdieu, Coleman, Putnam, and others, and explore its dialectical development. We redefine the new social capital as the function of mutual exchange and assistance possessed by the network of human relationships. It influences children's development through the neighbourhood community, and it is equipped with trust and discipline, the bases of democratic public life; a network beyond one's neighbourhood and community complements the function.

The reason we stick to places is simple: places are necessary for children grow up. Mammals are born from their mothers' wombs and cannot move immediately. According to zoologist A. Portmann, among animals, human babies spend the longest time sitting in their 'nests' (Portmann, 1956). After crawling, children start walking and then playing around the home, then they start joining the children playing on the street and expand their social spheres further by socialising as members of society.

Robin C. Moore proposed the idea of childhood domains, hierarchical stages in which children expand their scope of action as they develop (Moore, 1986). Earlier, he had vividly presented readers with children's interactions with their surroundings based on interviews using cognitive maps and children's guide tours, and this formed the basis of his concept of social ecology (Moore & Young, 1978), which had been based on Kevyn Lynch's works about people's psychological relationships with the environments (Lynch, 1960) including children growing up in cities (Lynch, 1977).

Children are the future human resources for the sustainability of society. Social capital tends to be concentrated in objects but it is more fundamentally irreplaceable by money; therefore, the future will differ depending on how it grows. The place of experience that is indispensable for growth is the place where children live in their growing years, and the place where you can live with support from the surrounding relationship. If an animal's nest is equivalent to a house, then the surroundings of the house are an important factor.

Furthermore, human beings have developed a complex system called society. To experience such social relationships in the process of growth requires a considerable amount of time and a variety of places of experience. This complex mechanism is cultivated through encounters with diverse people, including those on local streets, and through the interaction of one's own actions and reactions.

7. Children's participation and sustainable development

Against the backdrop of the 1989 Convention on the Rights of the Child and the theme of the 1992 Rio Global Environment Summit, sustainable development, UNICEF's Child Friendly Cities was proposed at HABITAT II held in Istanbul in 1996: 'Whether or not children are happy is proof of whether or not society is healthy and politics is going well'; the highest-priority item among its building blocks is child participation. The well-known Brundtland

Report described sustainable development as 'development that meets the needs of the present without compromising the ability of future generations to meet their own needs' (United Nations General Assembly, 1987). The definition by Japan's Ministry of Affairs, however, lacks the word 'ability'. The literal translation of the text provided by the Japanese government is as follows: 'development that satisfies the needs of the present while meeting the needs of future generations' (MOFA, 2003).

Here, the emphasis is clearly on the present. It lacks the perspective of developing human resources who can guarantee the abilities of future generations, maintain, and improve those abilities, share problems, and work together to solve problems. Ultimately, it lacks the perspective of lasting human security. For the sake of world peace and the continued development of democracy, community practice is fundamental to removing anxiety about the future and those concerning children. Thus, the formation of social capital through child-rearing has important implications for human security.

However, children are not just passive beings to be cared for. To create an environment in which children can grow up in a healthy manner and eliminate concerns about the future, they are also the subjects working with adults to address current issues. Articles 12 and 13 of the Convention on the Rights of the Child are therefore very important.

Roger Hart has played a global leadership role in child engagement since the founding of Child-Friendly Cities. At the request of UNICEF, he researched child participation efforts around the world and compiled a report that was later compiled into the book *Children's Participation* (Hart, 1997).

The UK has a long history of accumulating children's involvement. The term urban study, used by Patrick Geddes more than a century ago, had both the meaning of urban research by experts and the study of town by children. Edinburgh's Outlook Tower was a centre for urban study not only for adults but also for children (Geddes, 1915). The children's urban study was later taken over by the Town & Country Planning Association, and together with educators, the Urban Study Center was established. Colling Ward was a central figure; then Eileen Adams, a former art teacher, joined Colling Ward's Streetwork and contributed to the practice of children's participation in urban planning, linking education and urban planning (Adams & Ingham, 1998).

In addition, in collaboration with Kinoshita et al., authors exchanged information on Japanese–British *Urban Study* and child-involved urban planning and finalised it into a book called *Machi-Work* (Adams & Kinoshita, 2000). *Machi* means 'town' in Japanese, but it also means a community; streetwork could be considered machi-work in Japanese. Child participation in community design in Japan began with Kinoshita et al.'s three-generation's play maps in a residential area in Setagaya Ward, Tokyo (Kinoshita et al., 1982).

It was introduced in 'Children's Environmental Quarterly', edited by Robin Moore and Roger Hart (Kinoshita & Taishido Study Group, 1985/1984).

8. From the Bullerby model

Humans are social beings who live in relationships with others. The prototype of nests that live in groups is an environment like a village. In Astrid Lindgren's *Children of Bullerbyn Village*, six children in three houses play energetically and loudly. The adults around them and their various daily lives are simply depicted; this depicts the richness of social capital. Dr Marketta Kyttä, a professor at Aalto University in Finland, used independent mobility and affordances (environments that induce behaviour) as indexes of the richness of children's play environments, and the highest model of both indexes was a Bullerby model (Kyttä, 2003).

Based on Kyttä's model, we examined the hypothesis of the relationship between openness of spatial form, outdoor living, and social capital, as shown in Figure 2.2. We asked researchers and experts from six countries, including Dr Kyttä's laboratory to conduct survey about social capital raising children in each country. In Sweden, we surveyed a model district in Bullerbyn Village. In Scandinavia, green spaces, multigenerational shared recreational spaces, and freedom of movement have been shown to connect social capital for raising children. In Germany and Switzerland, cooperative residential areas are proven to offer rich social capital guaranteeing children's outdoor play. In urban development projects in the Netherlands and the United Kingdom, the continuity of green areas and open spaces have been ensured, thus ensuring the continuity of outdoor play spaces from the entrance of houses through shared spaces of streets. This has been pointed out as the spaces creating social capital that helps promoting children's outdoor play

Outdoor	**Private Garden** *Wasteland	**Community Space** *BULLERBY
Indoor	**Closed Room** *Cell	**Common Room** *Glasshouse
	Closed	Open

*Ref: Kytta(2003)

FIGURE 2.2 Indicators arranged from the Bullerby model.

We conducted a survey in Japan and compared the general trend of declining social capital in the neighbourhood and declining children's outdoor play between generations. We identified the usefulness of rich green areas and pedestrian-centred road networks for forming social capital. Declines in outdoor play and social capital can be seen even in rural areas now, but there are also examples of the influx of young households creating new connections between people, such as holding candy stores and markets.

9. From screen time to green time

Owing to the COVID-19 outbreak and the resulting lockdown, people began turning their attention to indoor spaces. The pandemic drove developments in IT that allowed for new phenomena such as working from home, online shopping, and increased online screen time, but efforts to control screen time and intentionally increase green time by going outside are also important for healthy lifestyles for both adults and children. If adults themselves go out and take action to improve the outdoor environment as a space to enjoy with children in their neighbourhood, children will see their backs and be forced to play outside.

In Japan, complaints about children's voices as noise are increasing. In the past, people often went outside, such as for meetings at the well on the street, sitting on the veranda and basking in the sun, and tending to the plants. However, today the relationships between neighbours have faded, homes have become closed, and insistence on quietness has become stronger. How can we solve the conflict between the elderly and children as symbolised by this noise problem? Local stakeholders should provide opportunities for face-to-face communication between children and complainants, for instance, including what they are doing with their days and how the noise is disturbing, and work together to come up with solutions.

Across Japan, some elderly participate in child-rearing support with the grandchildren of others; they are referred to as *tamago*, 'eggs' (他孫) of the community. In 2012, a group joined together in the Takayanagi-Kazehaya southern district of Kashiwa City and started multi-generational exchange salons they called 'tea salons' (茶論) that they promoted as 'local children, child-rearing generations, and the elderly all join hands to form one family'. Even others' grandchildren instinctively feel joy when the memories of elderly people are handed down. In the past, such relationships were built in and on semi-outdoor spaces such as porches, but the prospects for developing these spaces seem impossible in the current situation where housing is closed.

10. Conclusion: rebuilding social capital by creating playable outdoor spaces in living environments

Japan's measures against the declining birth rate have been symptomatic and lack decisive measures. In April 2023, the Children's Basic Law came into effect, and the Children's and Family Agency was established. As a countermeasure to the declining birth rate, Japan has periodically espoused 'give birth and multiply' and offered subsidies for having children. In Europe, children's rights are a given, and developed living environments where children can play and grow freely are far more advanced. Partnerships between the private sector and government are also progressing.

It is clear that human factors are important for children's play environments, such as playworkers and other service providers, not only physical settings. Mobile play such as play buses and outreach activities from adventure playgrounds and play centres coming to streets and parks would be useful for empowering local communities to rebuild social capital. It is necessary to enable children to participate in improving their play environments; interventions are needed to involve local communities in bringing children and families from indoors and gradually rebuilding social capital as child-rearing communities.

One way of building or restructuring social capital is inspecting the surrounding environment and considering whether it can be remodelled into a space where children can play but that adults can enjoy. Doing so creates neighbourhood environments that are both enjoyable and liveable, but what is the right way to go about it? From our collaborative study, we identified the technique of "pattern languages" (Alexander et al., 1977), for instance, neighbourhoods where children can be entrusted, open gardens, handmade roads for vehicles and pedestrians, living waterfronts, regenerating multigeneration housing complexes or residential area development that grows with children (refer to Chapter 11). Pattern languages contribute to creating spaces that enhance children's outdoor play and rebuild human connections from the level of children's living areas up to the block level. See Figures 2.3 and 2.4.

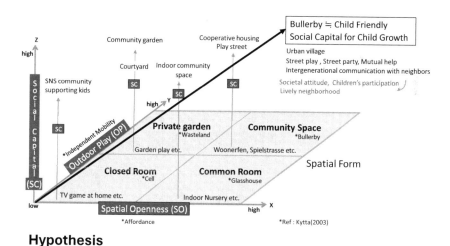

Hypothesis

FIGURE 2.3   3D diagram of spatial openness, social capital, and children's outdoor play.

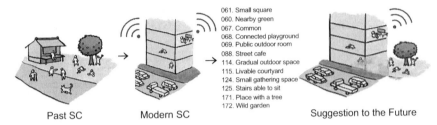

FIGURE 2.4 Transforming social capital and children's outdoor play.

Grant information

This work was supported by JSPS KAKENHI grant number JP20H02323.

References

Adams, E., & Ingham, S. (1998). *Changing places – children's participation in environmental planning*. The Children's Society.
Adams, E., & Kinoshita, I. (Eds.). (2000). *Machi-work – education for participation*. Fudo-sha.
Alexander, C., Ishikawa, S., & Silverstein, M. (1977). *A pattern language: Towns, buildings, construction*. Oxford Press.
Bourdieu, P. (1977). *Outline of a theory of practice*. Cambridge University Press.
Cabinet Office, Government of Japan. (2003). *Social capital: Seeking a virtuous cycle of rich human relationships and civic activities*. NPO Homepage. https://www.npo-homepage.go.jp/toukei/2009izen-chousa/2009izen-sonota/2002social-capital
Dewey, J. (1899). *The school and society*. University of Chicago.
Dubos, R. (1968). *So human an animal: How we are shaped by surroundings and events*. Scribner Book Company, Transaction Publishers 1998 edition. ISBN 0-7658-0429-8.
Dubos, R., & Ward, B. (1972). *Only one earth: The care and maintenance of a small planet, united nations conference on the human environment*. W W Norton & Co.
Geddes, P. (1915). *Cities in evolution*. Williams & Norgate.
Hart, R. (1997). *Children's participation – the theory and practice of involving young citizens in community development and environmental care*. UNICEF, Earthscan.
Jacobs, J. (1961). *The death and life of great American cities* (p. 82). Random House.
Kinoshita, I., Ogiwara, R., & Taishido Study Group. (1982). *Three generation's play maps, Kodomo no Asobi to Machi Kenkyukai*. Taishido Study Group.
Kinoshita, I., & Taishido Study Group. (1985). Neighborhood as childhood habitats. *Children's Environments Quarterly*, 1(4), 19–28. University of Cincinnati. (Original work published 1984, Winter)
Kyttä, M. (2003). *Children in outdoor contexts: Affordances and independent mobility in the assessment of environmental child friendliness*. Aalto University.
Lynch, K. (1960). *The image of the city*. MIT Press.
Lynch, K. (1977). *Growing up in cities*. MIT Press.
MOFA (Ministry of Foreign Affair Japan). (2003). Jizoku Kano Na Kaihatsu. *Sustainable Development*. https://www.mofa.go.jp/mofaj/gaiko/kankyo/wssd/wssd.html
Moore, R. C. (1986). *Childhood's domain: Play and place in child development*. Routledge.

Moore, R. C., & Young, D. (1978). Childhood outdoors: Toward a social ecology of the landscape. In I. Altman & J. F. Wholwill (Eds.), *Children and the environments, human behavior and environment* (pp. 83–130). Plenum Press.

Portmann, A. (1956). *Zoologie und das neue Bild des Menschen. Biologische Fragmente zu einer Lehre vom Menschen.* Rowohlt Verkag.

Putnam, R. D. (2000). *Bowling alone: The collapse and revival of American community.* Simon & Schuster.

Putnam, R. D., Leonardi, R., & Nanetti, R. Y. (1992). *Making democracy work: Civic traditions in modern Italy.* Princeton University Press.

United Nations General Assembly. (1987). *Our common future, chapter 2: Toward sustainable development, report of the world commission on environment and development.*

Ward, C. (1978). *The child in the city.* The Architectural Press, Ltd.

Ward, C., & Fyson, A. (1973). *Streetwork: The exploding school.* Routledge & K. Paul.

PART II
Cooperative and collective housing spaces

3

REQUIREMENTS FOR COMMUNITY AND INDIVIDUAL DEVELOPMENTS IN OUTDOOR SPACE DESIGN

From Freidorf, Switzerland

Urs Maurer

1. Historical context

In retrospect, the founding of an innovative cooperative housing complex in a small Swiss municipality in 1921 seems almost inevitable when one considers the wider historical context in which it took place.

As the catastrophe of the First World War drew to a close, the perception arose in many quarters of Europe that new ways of organising socioeconomic life were necessary. This need was so acutely felt that even the most radical of ideas, entailing the complete restructuring of society, were not only entertained but put into practice, with some seeking to form a stronger, more centralised, even totalitarian state, as manifested in fascism, socialism, and communism, and others seeking the destruction of the state as such and its replacement through the decentralisation of political and economic power, as manifested in the anarchist movement, with the so-called free mountains of the Swiss alpine canton of Jura being a notable example. It is from within this context that the project which would come to be known as Freidorf can be evaluated and appreciated in terms of its vision and practical realisation.

2. Sources of inspiration

The concept of Freidorf drew inspiration from both traditional ideas and contemporary innovations in two seemingly unrelated fields: socioeconomics and pedagogy. The cooperative movement of the late 19th century, which was largely developed and put into practice in various parts of England, bore a noticeable similarity to the Alemannic Swiss tradition of the *Allmende*, the commons, under which farmland and forest of value to the community was held in common but managed under private initiative. Thus, the principle of cooperation was seen as a "third way" between capitalism and socialism/communism.

The pedagogical movement, as begun by J.J. Rousseau (1712–1778), more than a century earlier and continued by H. Pestalozzi (1746–1827), F. Fröbel (1782–1852), and J. Dewey (1858–1952), envisioned an educational program which valued the growth and development of children and adults over time as a means of both adapting to and improving society. Pestalozzi developed a three-circle model that considered the education of parents and the education of children to be inseparable; for this reason, all adult residents in the Freidorf were obliged to participate in at least one working group. In addition to topics relating to the self-administration of the village, there were also cultural groups, such as a group that focused on child education using Pestalozzi's book *Lienhard and Gertrud*, a novel Pestalozzi published in four volumes from 1771 to 1778; as an alternative to the individual development novel, Pestalozzi created the paradigm of the German folk novel with collective conflicts and utopian solutions. Economic independence through cooperation and social improvement through life-long education and cultivation thus became the two lenses through which the vision of the Freidorf project came into focus.

3. Radical political ideas and concept: free from mortgage debt

The name Freidorf itself – which translates literally as 'free village' – indicates one of the most radical ideas the project sought to realise: the establishment and development of a community entirely free from mortgage debt. The land, the private houses, the public buildings, the streets, the parks, the fountains, the gardens – the entire project was to be, from its inception, debt free. The vision of economic independence was to be realised by a combination of private initiative and common cooperation, whereby the practical goal was self-sufficiency to the greatest possible degree, both for individuals and for the community.

Every townhouse in Freidorf was planned with an adjoining private garden. In addition to this, two community gardens for planting vegetables and berries were planned, as well as a row of nut trees. Space for a large park was reserved in the centre of the complex to be used by children at play as well as by the entire community for public events, but it could be used for agricultural projects in times of need, as was the case during the Second World War, when it was used to farm potatoes.

The large community centre housed a cooperative shop offering not only the necessities of life such as bread, milk, cheese, and beer, but also non-consumables such as shoes and clothes, produced in cooperatives located in the wider region. It also offered recreational opportunities, such as a bowling alley and a theatre with stage, a laundry, and a restaurant, as well

Community and individual development in outdoor space design 33

as a wide range of adult educational opportunities, conference rooms, and a grand hall which could seat some five hundred people. Other innovative ideas realised by Freidorf include cooperative insurance and pension programs, and – perhaps most radical of all – an independent and self-sustaining alternative monetary system.

4. 'A project of national interest'

Needless to say, the potential for socio-economic change represented by the Freidorf concept was tremendous. The key to unlocking that potential came in the form of 7,500,000 Swiss francs, taken from the federal treasury's war profits tax fund, which in today's money would easily be valued at over 50 times that amount. Freidorf was undertaken as a pilot project of national interest with the potential to revolutionise social life, not merely as an example but as a concrete first step: the agreement with the government stipulated that the inhabitants were to pay into a common fund that after accumulating for 25 years would be used to found another, similarly planned and constructed, cooperative community. The two communities would then save to found another two, and then another four, etc., yielding 16 debt-free communities in 100 years, housing some 8,000 people. Figures 3.1 to 3.27 give a visual overview of how Freidorf operated.

5. A picture report from the pioneering era and the time of economic crises

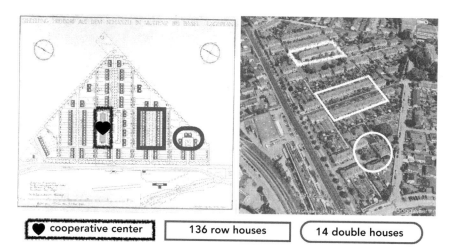

FIGURES 3.1 & 3.2 Relatively large, comfortable houses for 150 families, each with an electricity supply. In the middle of the triangular settlement, there is a huge communal centre.

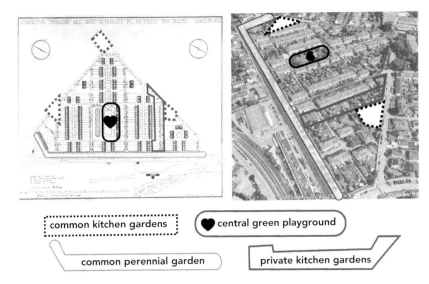

FIGURES 3.3 & 3.4   Concerning our main topic, the outdoor space, there are not only very big private and two shared kitchen gardens but also a great communal playground and an extensive perennial garden, as a special concern of the architect, Hannes Meyer.

FIGURES 3.5 & 3.6   The central playground was and still is an important fairgrounds and playground for both children and adults and is regularly watered and turned into an icefield in wintertime.

The revolutionary idea of Freidorf was the financing system that was not based on repayable or interest-bearing loan money, but on donations or endowments, a concept that should have given impetus to the international cooperative movement.

The 7,500,000 SFr. to construct Freidorf was financed by the state in the form of a waiver of the war profits tax. In return, a fund was to be created from the rents for land, residential buildings, the community centre, and

FIGURE 3.7 International Co-operative Day, July 1924.

FIGURE 3.8 Students doing gymnastics on the almost traffic-free street in front of the community centre.

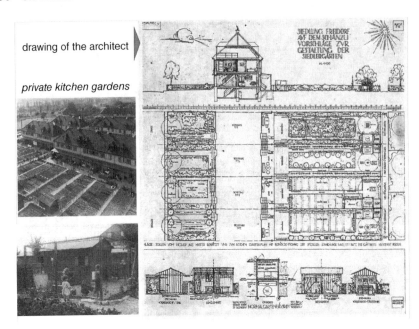

FIGURES 3.9, 3.10, & 3.11 The private kitchen gardens are the basis for the self-sufficiency of families as the innermost circle of society according to the model of the Swiss pedagogue Heinrich Pestalozzi. The planting plans were drawn not by a gardener but at the hand of the architect.

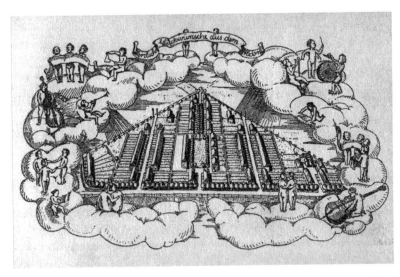

FIGURE 3.12 A postcard from Hannes Meyer for the 1924 ceremony. Freidorf saw itself as a place of peace and harmony, a paradise on earth.

Community and individual development in outdoor space design **37**

FIGURE 3.13 The architect: Hannes Meyer.

FIGURE 3.14 The ally: Edmund Schulthess, federal president (top right).

38 Urs Maurer

FIGURE 3.15   The three guests of honour: Edmund Schulthess (left); G.J.D.C. Goedhard, president of International Federation of Cooperatives (middle), the initiator, Bernhard Jäggi.

FIGURE 3.16   7,500,000 Swiss francs from the treasury of the federal war profits tax.

Community and individual development in outdoor space design 39

FIGURE 3.17   1921 carnival of Basle freedom fight of drunken villagers.

FIGURE 3.18   The huge cooperative house called the 'temple of community'.
Source: Hannes Meyer.

40 Urs Maurer

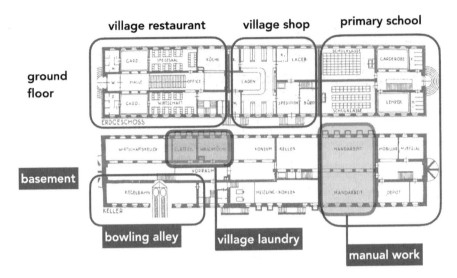

FIGURE 3.19 The uses on the ground floor and in the basement of the community building.

FIGURES 3.20 & 21 The primary school and village shop; clothes and shoes could be bought in addition to everyday goods.

FIGURES 3.22 & 23 Restaurant on the ground floor and bowling alley in the basement.

Community and individual development in outdoor space design 41

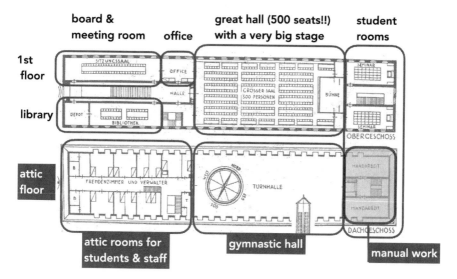

FIGURE 3.24   The uses on the first floor and the attic floor of the community building.

FIGURE 3.25   The hall with 500 seats with restaurant seating is the largest in the entire region. In addition to school and popular theatre, avant-garde dance, and puppet theatre were performed on the stage, as they were performed at the Bauhaus in Dessau.

FIGURE 3.26 While the common planting areas are still used for vegetables, fruit and berries, the private kitchen gardens have become lawn playgrounds and flower gardens.

FIGURE 3.27 The original undivided lawn has been equipped with all-weather playgrounds. Here, temporarily set up tables and benches on a second-hand market.

infrastructure, which was expected to make it possible to finance a second debt-free village after about 25 years.

The architect Hannes Meyer characterised the central cooperative building as a mixture between a factory building, a monastery, and a temple.

6. Freidorf today after more than sixty years of economic boom

In the meantime, apartments for the elderly have been built on the adjacent reserve Freidorf land, and the Freidorf shop has become a modern cooperative supermarket.

7. Eigenheimstrasse/heimatstrasse, a free association in Zürich from 1979

Built in 1892 as one of the first cooperatives in the city of Zurich, the flats at Eigenheimstrasse/Heimatstrasse were later privatised. Something of the cooperative spirit remained, so that the residents initiated and politically enforced one of the city's first residential streets in 1979. A residential street means that cars are tolerated for emergency access but are only allowed to drive a maximum of 20 kilometres per hour (Figures 3.28 and 3.29). The children in the neighbourhood play and their mothers have a lot of contact and organise joint meals and street parties (Figures 3.30 and 3.32).

FIGURE 3.28   Heavily traffic-calmed streets with seats and flower pots, midst in the city.

44 Urs Maurer

FIGURE 3.29   Privately owned land and buildings with a strong club organisation.

FIGURES 3.30 & 31   St. Nicholas welcomes the children on the street.

8. Erlenmatt-East, a 2021 cooperative district in Basel

In 2021, in the city of Basel, a cooperatively organised, dense urban district called Erlenmatt (Figure 3.33) was created on a converted railway and industrial area with generous, communally used open space (Figure 3.34).

Community and individual development in outdoor space design   **45**

FIGURE 3.32   A jazz concert on the street.

FIGURE 3.33   Aerial view of Erlenmatt.

The new residential quarter is exemplary in terms of social, ecological, and economic sustainability. Social here stands for participation, freedom of traffic, and outdoor spaces that can be used in a variety of ways and lively neighbourhood relationships. Ecological refers to the fact that residents use a maximum of 2,000 watts per person and day and photovoltaics. Figures 3.33 to 3.43 show signs of life around Erlenmatt.

46 Urs Maurer

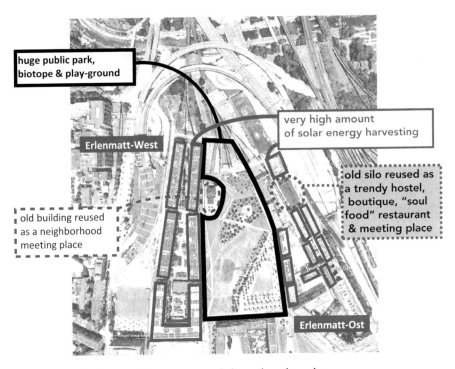

FIGURE 3.34 Erlenmatt's layout around the railroad tracks.

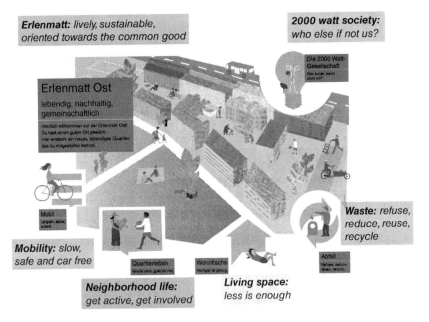

FIGURE 3.35 Principles of Erlenmatt in operation.

Community and individual development in outdoor space design   **47**

FIGURES 3.36–39   The association organises regular events.

FIGURES 3.40–43   Kindergarteners making active contact with plants by growing vegetables, berries, and fruit, as well as with chickens.

Four strong, successful, politically active institutions stand behind this pioneering project: a foundation called Habitat; a cooperative called Cooperative Erlenmatt for the user financing; an association called Verein Erlenmatt, for organising meetings, events, and neighbourly help; and a public welfare pension fund called Abendroth. Without these strong private and public institutions, this major project would not have been possible and would hardly have been successful in the long term (Figure 3.44).

9. The developmental stages of human consciousness from early history to the present and near future

The German cultural historian and anthropologist Jean Gebser (1905–1973) wrote his main work, *Origin and Presence*, during the Second World War in exile in the small Swiss town of Burgdorf and published it in 1953. Although Ken Wilber developed and differentiated them, I use Jean Gebser's simpler terms, which are more firmly anchored in common parlance. In Figure 3.45, Summarisation of Gebser's five levels of consciousness with reference to the senses and spatial perception by the author.

10. The four phases of child development of consciousness and the corresponding outdoor furnishings

Based on my research, I've concluded that every child experiences four qualities of consciousness during their development. As presented in Figure 3.46, specific senses, activities, and spatial experiences take centre stage in each of these phases of a child's development. For instance, the difficult phase of puberty requires special attention: young people want to be with their peers but at the same time need clear boundaries, attention, and convincing, experienced leaders. Meanwhile, as displayed in Figure 3.47, when designing children's playgrounds, these different phases and associated needs should be differentiated. Figures 3.48 and 3.49 show a KITA facility in Zurich that combines commercial and residential facilities. Figures 3.50 and 3.51 show KITA Storchennest in St. Gallen Rhine, offering children a more natural experience.

11. Six conclusions

I've drawn a number of conclusions from my research. First, I believe the term "child" is much too diffuse; we have to distinguish at least four different developmental phases of childhood. Second, the crisis of puberty requires special attention and mindfulness from teachers, social workers, and spatial

Community and individual development in outdoor space design 49

× Geschäftsleitung

Klaus Hubmann
Geschäftsführer

Jochen Brodbeck
Leiter Bauprojekte, Mitglied der Geschäftsleitung

Sonja Fritschi
Leiterin Personalwesen & Zentrale Dienste, Mitglied der Geschäftsleitung

Raphael Schicker
Leiter Projektentwicklung, Mitglied der Geschäftsleitung

Isgard Tosch
Leiter Bewirtschaftung, Mitglied der Geschäftsleitung

personal engagement

× Projektentwicklung

Raphael Schicker
Leiter Projektentwicklung, Mitglied der Geschäftsleitung

Urs Buomberger
Projektentwickler, Berufsbildner

Nikola Karadzic
Projektentwickler

Community work of several organizations

o *Habitat (foundation)*
o *PK Abendroth (pension fund)*
o *Verein Erlenmatt (association)*
o *Genossenschaft Erlenmatt (cooperative)*

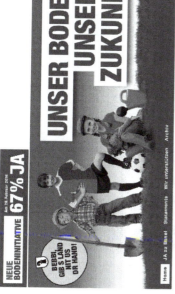

FIGURE 3.44 The four strong institutions behind the Erlenmatt Ost project.

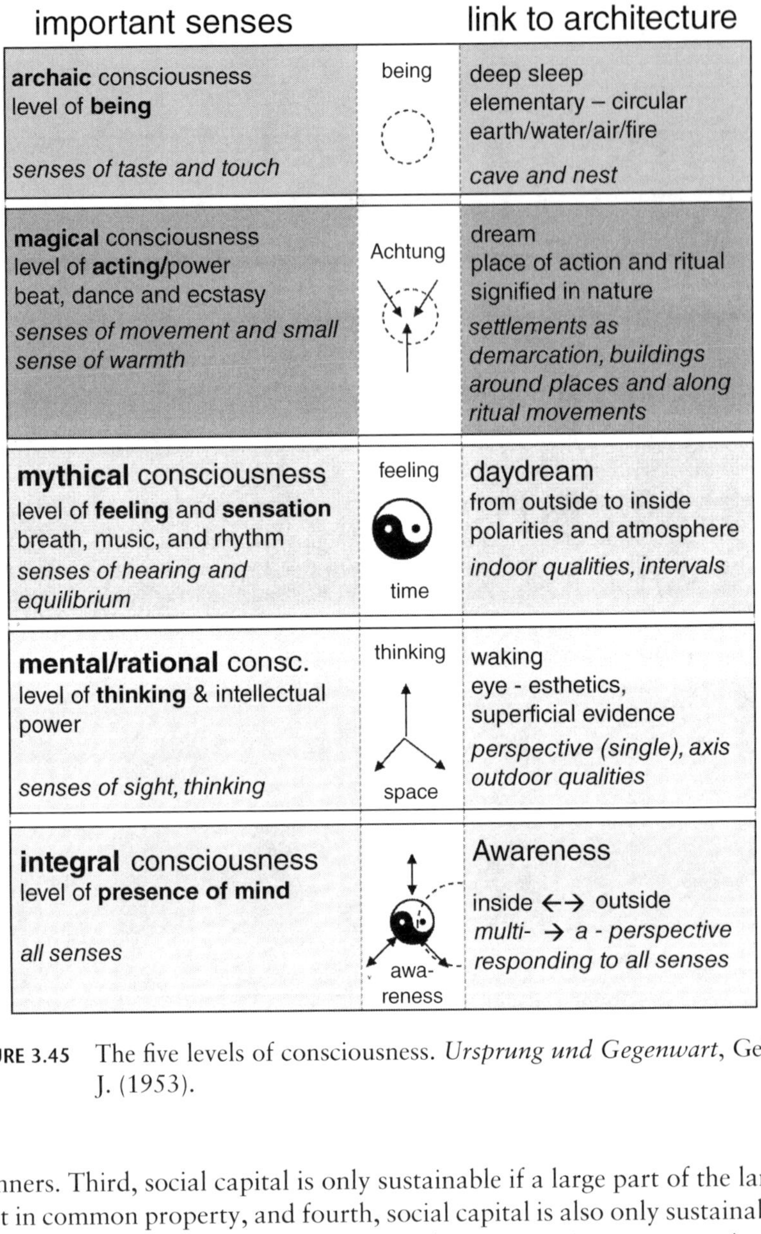

50 Urs Maurer

important senses		link to architecture
archaic consciousness level of **being** *senses of taste and touch*	being	deep sleep elementary – circular earth/water/air/fire *cave and nest*
magical consciousness level of **acting**/power beat, dance and ecstasy *senses of movement and small sense of warmth*	Achtung	dream place of action and ritual signified in nature *settlements as demarcation, buildings around places and along ritual movements*
mythical consciousness level of **feeling** and **sensation** breath, music, and rhythm *senses of hearing and equilibrium*	feeling time	daydream from outside to inside polarities and atmosphere *indoor qualities, intervals*
mental/rational consc. level of **thinking** & intellectual power *senses of sight, thinking*	thinking space	waking eye - esthetics, superficial evidence *perspective (single), axis outdoor qualities*
integral consciousness level of **presence of mind** *all senses*	awa- reness	Awareness inside ←→ outside multi- → a - perspective *responding to all senses*

FIGURE 3.45 The five levels of consciousness. *Ursprung und Gegenwart*, Gebser, J. (1953).

planners. Third, social capital is only sustainable if a large part of the land is kept in common property, and fourth, social capital is also only sustainable if it is organised through legal structures such as associations, cooperatives, or foundations. Related to these, social capital is only sustainable if the neighbourhood is inhabited by two to three generations from the beginning. Sixth and finally, increasing outdoor quality for children, parents, and elder people increases social capital in neighbourhoods.

Community and individual development in outdoor space design 51

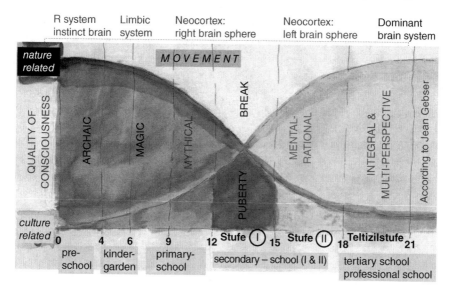

FIGURE 3.46 The four phases of child development as four qualities of consciousness. *Den Schulbau neu denken, fühlen und wollen. Erneuerung der Fundamente, Entwicklung von Leitbildern und Perspektiven jenseits der Moderne.* Maurer, U. (2007).

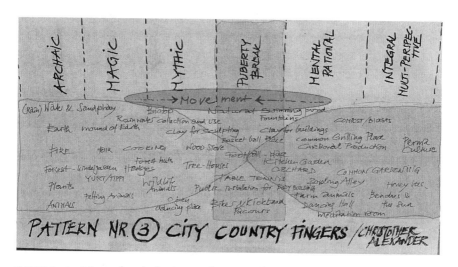

FIGURE 3.47 Notes for designing a playground according to Gebser's five levels of consciousness.

FIGURE 3.48 A daycare centre in the city of Zurich in an ordinary residential and commercial building.

FIGURE 3.49 On the 'garden side' of KITA, not a single parking space is 'sacrificed' for the children's needs.

FIGURE 3.50 Children don't need much more than a safe, natural place with a few facilities.

FIGURE 3.51 Einstein said that 'playing is the highest form of research'.

Grant information

This work was supported by JSPS KAKENHI Grant Number JP20H02323.

References

25 Jahre Freidorfgenossenschaft. (1943, August).
50 Jahre Siedlungsgenossenschaft Freidorf. (1919–1969).
100 Jahre: Das Freidorf. Die Genossenschaft. Leben in einer aussergewöhnlichen Siedlung. Bolliger, C. et al. (2019). Christoph Merian Verlag.
Gebser, J. (1953). *Ursprung & Gegenwart*.
Kieren, M. (1990). *Hannes Meyer, Architekt, Dokumente zur Frühzeit 1919–1927*. Verlag Arthur Niggli AG.
Maurer, U. (1995). *75 Jahre Leben im Freidorf. Zur 75-jährigen Siedlungsgeschichte*.
Maurer, U. (2007). *Den Schulbau neu denken, fühlen und wollen. Erneuerung der Fundamente, Entwicklung von Leitbildern und Perspektiven jenseits der Moderne* [Doctorate thesis, faculteit bouwkunde Nr. 121, TU Eindhoven].
Maurer, U. (2017). *Den Schulbau neu denken, fühlen und wollen*. In Weyland, B. & Watschinger, J. (Eds.), *Lernen und Raum entwickeln*. Klinkhardt Verlag.

4

ACKERMANNBOGEN IN MUNICH, A MODERN, CHILD-FRIENDLY URBAN VILLAGE

Kati Landsiedel

1. Introducing the site: Ackermannbogen

Ackermannbogen (Figure 4.1) is a housing project of approximately 40 ha located in the north-west of the city of Munich. It accommodates 7,000 people. It was built in four stages, beginning in 2002 and concluding in 2014 (wagnis eG, 2023).

The first building stages were initiated as a public urban development measure. In the following stages, joint building ventures erected some of the housing units; future residents pooled their financial resources, but also their plans and ideas for the housing projects. In the final stage, the non-profit collective housing cooperative wagnis eG took over to build the last blocks. In short, most of the housing project was planned and built in a bottom-up, resident-driven process.

The whole area and especially the wagnis cooperative is characterised by a good mix of state-aided and privately financed housing that leads to an exceptional social mix in residents: following the city requirements of the so-called Munich Model, one third of the apartments must be social housing for people with low income who receive state assistance. The wagnis buildings are rented out following the cooperative model: when you become a member, you pay a relatively low rent. Members are chosen following a certain ratio of social groups. The housing units that were built by the joint building venture groups are privately financed and owned.

Residents highly value personal well-being. Overall, they report that they especially benefit from good quality of living in a lively and active neighbourhood with a low fluctuation rate, low ancillary costs due to self-management, and a variety of traffic-free, human-friendly, green, and healthy communal

DOI: 10.4324/9781003456223-6

FIGURE 4.1 Finding your way to the many community spaces in the Ackermannbogen. Photograph by Ute Haas.

spaces. The planning of the area had the needs of future residents as a high priority and therefore provides a range of features that are known for increasing living quality.

The site comprises several kindergartens, nurseries, daycare centers and a youth center to provide safe spaces for children and young people. Residents are not encouraged to own cars, since there is a very good public transport connection. Also, most of the roads are play streets or no traffic areas.

There are a variety of public spaces, outdoors as well as indoors, with a range of different meeting places like cafés, restaurants, little parks, a village plaza, and areas with benches. Almost one quarter (9.5 ha) of the area consists of gardens and grasslands, and of course there are playgrounds for different age groups (Figure 4.2).

Another special factor in Ackermannbogen is the very active Neighborly Help Association (NHA; Nachbarschaftshilfe). This organisation is a neighbourhood meeting point and networking partner for all neighbours in Ackermannbogen regardless of social and national origin, age, gender or

Ackermannbogen in Munich, a child-friendly urban village 57

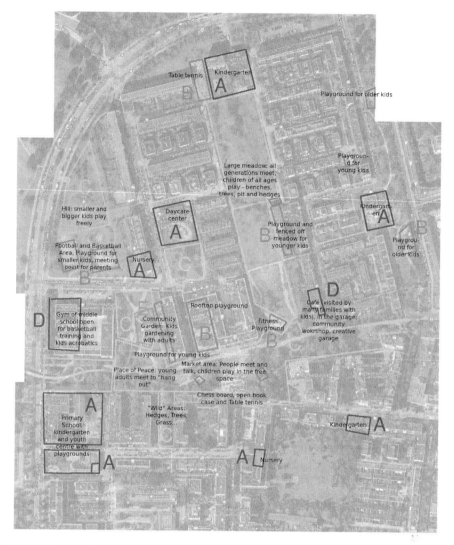

FIGURE 4.2 Ackermannbogen from the air with its community spaces for children. A: daycare; B: playgrounds, C: free space, D: indoor community space, E: community garden.

Source: Google Earth, Image © 2023 GeoContent, Maxar Technologies, Map Data © 2023 GeoBasis-DE/BKG (© 2009), edited by the author.

religion, especially for neighbours with disabilities. It coordinates a lot of the quarter's activities, takes up concerns and topics from the neighbourhood, strengthens and supports community-promoting initiatives, helps with questions relating to neighbourhoods and housing, and invites people to get involved. The NHA offers rooms on different sites with various purposes and runs the community garden as an open-air neighbourhood meeting place. Most of the activities run on neighbourhood-based voluntary resident work (Ackermannbogen eV, 2023).

A wide range of hands-on activities for children, young people, and adults offer a wealth of opportunities to meet like-minded people and expand the neighbourhood network. Whether it's creative and health offers for adults, playful and musical offers for children, learning aids for pupils, repair cafés, or action days for everyone, the Nachbarschaftshilfe is a contact point for all neighbours and (almost) all concerns.

Of the 7,000 residents, 23% are children and youth. This is a very high share of children compared with the city's average of 15.1% (Stadt München, 2023); this could be because children and families were consistently considered in the planning of the site. The houses are mostly bigger buildings with many units, and there are only few smaller multi-family houses; there are no single-family homes; as a result, much free space remains between buildings. Furthermore, planners chose to make most of the traffic areas car free. Daycare centres, playgrounds, and free play spaces were included in the planning from the beginning.

The residents consider Ackermannbogen an urban village. Unlike in many other parts of the city, residents know about 50–100 of their neighbours. The everyday life is described as very social; when people go out, you almost always stop to chat on the street. Services to meet all daily needs are in walking distance, like shops, supermarkets, gardens, schools, and daycare centres, recreation and sports areas, cafés and restaurants, and a weekly farmer's market. This also encourages personal encounters in public spaces because you spend more time within the neighbourhood itself.

Additionally, mutual help is common. To give just two examples, parents take the initiative to help each other at the daycare centres, and the NHA organises a wide range of neighbourly help. The association's activities are tailored to what residents need because the residents take the planning initiative. The NHA is described as very lively and valuable, especially during the COVID-19 pandemic lockdowns in 2020–2022, when elderly people and families were in dire need of support.

2. Where do kids play?

Before investigating the ways and opportunities for kids to gain social capital at Ackermannbogen, I want to have a look at the spaces where children spend their time away from home. Kids at Ackermannbogen have a host of play spaces to choose from: daycare centres (Figure 4.3), designated playgrounds, free or undefined spaces, indoor community spaces, and the community garden.

FIGURE 4.3   One of the Ackermannbogen daycare centres. Photograph by the author.

Daycare centres

School hours in Germany usually only comprise the morning hours, especially for primary school kids. Since parents often work until later in the evening there is a need for childcare in the afternoon. This is mostly implemented in daycare centres, where kids can be supervised until up to 5 pm. Kindergartens and nurseries usually offer supervision the whole day, depending on the families' situation. All childcare institutions have a garden attached to them.

Youth centres offer indoor and outdoor spaces for children and youth of primary and secondary school age. They usually open from lunchtime to around 6 pm and later on weekends and provide safe spaces for special activities or for just hanging out and courses that are adapted to the visitor's interests. Ackermannbogen has a primary and a middle school, three kindergartens, two nurseries, a daycare centre, and a youth centre. All institutions are reachable by bike or on foot, so it's safe for older children to make their way alone if needed.

Designated playgrounds

Ackermannbogen comprises 11 designated playground areas for different age groups. There are four areas especially dedicated to sports: a table tennis area,

FIGURE 4.4   The hill playground. Photograph by the author.

a football area, a volleyball and basketball area, and a fitness playground. The football field is equipped with a rededicated shipping container with wooden benches, so young adults have a place to hang out on rainy days. There is a rooftop playground with various parkour units and various areas with play structures for kids of different ages. Next to the central grassland, there is also a fenced-off meadow area as a safe space for the smallest children. Figures 4.4 and 4.5 show two of the playgrounds at Ackermannbogen,

Free spaces

As I've described, there are vast free spaces between the houses in Ackermannbogen. The core of the compound is a big meadow, about 2 ha in size, shown in Figure 4.6. The large meadow provides space for ball games, kite flying, running, doing yoga, and the like. Children of all generations play here, and adults come to accompany their children or to pursue their own activities. The space is bordered with benches, so it invites elderly people to linger, too. The northern part of the meadow has an elongated pit seamed with hedges that make great spots for hide-and-seek and other games. To the eastern part of Ackermannbogen, there is a hill-like structure that harbours the quarter's geothermic facility. The hill is a great place for free play year-round and sledding in winter.

FIGURE 4.5 The fitness playground. Photograph by the author.

FIGURE 4.6 The big meadow at Ackermannbogen. Photograph by the author.

While the building was still in process in the area, children also used the construction sites or their surroundings as playgrounds. This has now stopped due to the completion of the works, but some wild areas remain – sites with natural growth and shrubbery that facilitate free play and building of tree houses and hideouts.

Indoor community spaces

A specialty of Ackermannbogen are the community rooms in the cooperative's houses; you can book them for birthday parties, family events, flea markets, workshops, etc. There are three such rooms distributed over the buildings in the area. The gym of the middle school can be used by sports groups. There is a privately organised basketball training and a kids acrobatics team.

Community garden

A jewel of the project is the community garden, the so-called *Stadtacker* ('city acre'; Figure 4.7); it is mostly run by resident volunteers. The group offers programs for school classes who can maintain their own garden beds under the supervision of gardening experts. There is also a nature kids group that

FIGURE 4.7 The community garden at Ackermannbogen. Photograph by Ute Haas.

meets in the garden for various nature education activities run by a resident who is a member of a regional nature organisation.

3. Where do kids gain social capital?

As seen in previous chapters, building social capital requires giving children a social environment that helps them play safely outside with friends, interact with adults in the community, and grow as members of society. At Ackermannbogen, kids have many options for contact with other children and people of different generations. They live in a lively neighbourhood where they experience mutual help in wide social networks. They have contact with nature and can widely appropriate their own safe and diverse play spaces. Every social interaction; every joint venture with other people; and every meetup with peers, adults, or elderly can be a possibility for building social capital. Having reviewed the spaces where kids roam in Ackermannbogen, I now focus on the how they help to build social capital.

Contact with other children

As I noted, kids have plenty of contact with other children at Ackermannbogen. They meet their school friends at daycare centres or on playgrounds. Pathways are short between the common areas (Figure 4.8), so children can

FIGURE 4.8   Kids playing on the footpath. Photograph by Ute Haas.

FIGURE 4.9 Contact between generations. Photograph by the author.

go to the playgrounds often and by themselves and are independent of their caregivers to accompany them. Even for smaller kids, playgrounds and play spaces are close by so the thresholds for parents to go out with them are low.

Other generations and other cultures

The inviting and inclusive character of all spaces at Ackermannbogen encourages many generations to be outside, so kids get into contact with a variety of other age groups (Figure 4.9). Families meet casually at playgrounds, while shopping, or in the community spaces, forming friendships in the process.

There is a residence for elderly on the compound which regrettably is fenced off from the public spaces, but the contact between younger and older generations works well in the community garden, where older people teach younger ones. Intergenerational play also takes place at the giant chess board on one of the playgrounds and in the monthly bike repair workshop where grownups serve as models for kids.

There are generally many families in Ackermannbogen; they were a special focus in building the project. There is also a focus on international as well as intergenerational residents: 21% are of non-German nationality, and people from a total of 46 different countries live in the area. This openness to the world was also vital to the planners; in the compound, there are guest rooms

FIGURE 4.10 A neighbourhood festival. Photograph by Ute Haas.

that can be rented to accommodate guests. Furthermore, all public spaces and most of the houses were built to be accessible for disabled persons, equipped with wide entrance doors, elevators, etc., so there are opportunities for kids to see and accept forms of handicap in the people around them. Figure 4.10 shows a neighbourhood festival, one of the common community activities at Ackermannbogen.

Mutual help and social networks

Kids at Ackermannbogen experience mutual help and support from neighbours, although the NHA is key to all neighbourly activities. It organises a range of events and activities that all residents are invited to participate in: expositions, workshops, dance classes and many more. The program booklet for six months usually comprises 60 pages.

Furthermore, the NHA engages in educational activities especially for kids. There is a German–Japanese play group, gardening activities for kids, play buses, and a children's art school, the School of Fantasy. There are many events focusing on children's and families' needs like jumble sales for children's clothes (Figure 4.11), clothes swaps, kids' playgroups, homework help groups, and a special project to simplify parent's supervisions of their children's way to school, the Bus on Its Feet: neighbours form groups of children who have a similar way to school, and parents take turns accompanying them until they are independent enough to go alone.

FIGURE 4.11   A children's jumble sale. Photograph by Ute Haas.

Because there are many families in Ackermannbogen, many residents with small kids naturally form strong social networks. Parents meet and connect at the care institutions (kindergarten, daycare centres) or playgrounds and successively build up personal friendships. Another factor that fosters the building of social networks is the cooperative housing model, which attracts people with prosocial dispositions who are comfortable sharing, a healthy background for kids to experience and gain social capital. An iconic example for this disposition is the book share shelf on the market plaza: people bring books they have read and can take new ones out. The shelf is cared for by a group of volunteers, and there has been no vandalism so far.

Contact with nature and wide appropriation of play spaces

As discussed previously, kids living at Ackermannbogen have a host of possibilities to go outside and have nature experiences simply because suitable areas are close by. They are also able to appropriate spaces and convert them into play areas even if they are not designated areas for kids. This is partially because children are an accepted portion of the population in this area because there are many families with similar needs around. But there are also two other factors at work here: safety and diversity of play (Figures 4.12 and 4.13).

FIGURE 4.12   Building play shelters. Photograph by Ute Haas.

FIGURE 4.13   Water play. Photograph by Ute Haas.

Safe possibilities of movement and play

Most of the area is free of car traffic, which makes it relatively safe for children to reach or appropriate play spaces on their own. There are many wide, open areas that make it possible for kids to run free with minimal intervention by their parents, who can watch them from afar.

Diverse possibilities for play

Ackermannbogen provides many different possibilities for play, making it interesting for kids with different needs or preferences. In the area, you can find the different playgrounds; fountains; and diverse terrain formations like the hill, the pit, the meadow, and the hedges. There are the various sports areas for football, volleyball, and table tennis as well as the fitness playground, and the NHA's manifold cultural and creative programmes provide facilities such as rooms for band rehearsals. In short, people of different ages and with different interests can all find suitable spaces for themselves in the Ackermannbogen.

4. How does housing influence children's play?

Now I focus on the relationship between architectural planning and children's play in Ackermannbogen. I examine the characteristics of the play spaces of Ackermannbogen and understand how they facilitate play. Seven factors are salient, and I discuss them in more detail here.

Diverse playgrounds

The diversity of playgrounds is important for attracting kids of all age groups, needs, and interests. It is crucial to have areas with multiple purposes to bring different groups into contact with each other as well as having designated play areas where kids and their parents can have safe spaces for play. This is implemented at Ackermannbogen very well, with playgrounds for different age groups as well as undefined spaces for appropriation by different users.

Open green spaces

Compared with other city areas, Ackermannbogen has little to no asphalt and a large share of open and green spaces (Figure 4.14). In addition to other physical and psychological benefits, this facilitates children's play by giving them the means to explore natural spaces largely on their own.

Diverse terrain formations

Ackermannbogen provides diverse terrains and geographic features like ditches, meadows, hedges, and groups of trees as well as the hill (Figure 4.15).

Ackermannbogen in Munich, a child-friendly urban village 69

FIGURE 4.14 Open space. Photograph by the author.

FIGURE 4.15 Diverse terrains. Photograph by Ute Haas.

FIGURE 4.16 Undefined Space. Photograph by the author.

This also enables play by giving a host of stimuli. In particular, little hills, pits, and hedges facilitate autonomous and discovery play, when kids can hide from the view of grownups.

Undefined spaces

There are designated playgrounds at Ackermannbogen but also many undefined spaces (Figure 4.16). Here, kids can make up their own games or use structures in new ways, like making a cut tree into a climbing bar, playing with the water fountain in summer, or building hideouts in hedges. This stimulates children's fantasy and autonomy in a playful way.

Continuity of space between houses and outdoors

An important facilitating factor at Ackermannbogen is the continuity of space between homes and outdoor areas. Kids just open the door and are outside, and a playground is always in walking distance. This is especially true for the apartments on the ground floor, but residents on other levels also benefit from the closeness of play spaces (Figure 4.17).

FIGURE 4.17 Continuity between home and play spaces. Photograph by the author.

No cars

In most of the Ackermannbogen areas, there is no car traffic, so they need minimal supervision and no protection from traffic hazards. This enables kids to go play on their own and leads to more possibilities for play since less supervision and time from parents is needed (Figure 4.18).

Few to no fences

Ackermannbogen is also characterised by wide spaces with few to no fences. Kids can move around freely and appropriate almost all of the public area.

5. What are obstacles to kids' play?

The Ackermannbogen project is widely seen as a success by its residents. It has been called a successful 'paradise for kids and families'. There is however no untroubled paradise, and conflicts occur at Ackermannbogen. As everywhere, there are some people who are not terribly fond of kids, so there can be complaints about noise and about youth 'existing' in places designated for the elderly. This is partially because the project did not incorporate facilities

FIGURE 4.18 Areas free of car traffic. Photograph by the author.

for older youth in the planning and execution as for younger children. As a result, there are too few spaces for young adults to hang out and be on their own.

However, such criticisms remain exceptions. Since the area was built as a family housing project, most people knew what they were buying into and are okay with kids around. Additionally, there will always be groups that choose to not use the possibilities that their architectural surroundings offer. Depending on age and individual priorities or development stages, they might still spend their time on computer games or other indoor activities. It is nevertheless important that opportunities for outdoor play and building up social capital exist.

6. Arguments and cases for social capital and child growth in Germany

In this last section, I introduce a local planning tool, the Catalog of Criteria for Child and Youth Conform Building and Planning (Landeshauptstadt München, 2000), that incorporates principles and concrete questions for different levels of planning, namely urban development plans, zoning plans, construction plans, and practical use cases (e. g. house rules or park rules).

This catalogue encompasses six sections that have to be considered in planning processes: 1) kids have rights of their own, 2) security and health, 3) usability, 4) flexibility, 5) participation, and 6) experience and diversity. In the final section of this chapter, I compare the measures taken at Ackermannbogen against the catalogue criteria.

1. Kids have rights of their own

- Are children's needs (play, mobility, space, diversity) incorporated in the planning instruments?
- Are institutions that promote children's rights involved in the planning?

Since future residents were asked to participate in most the planning during the Ackermannbogen building process, children's needs were probably incorporated via the contributions of the families. However, there was no report of children directly participating in the planning process. As there are many children's facilities on the site, it can be assumed that some institutions that would speak up for children's needs and rights were heard in the planning.

2. Security and health

- Are dangers to physical or psychological health of children (emissions, soil contamination, noise, traffic) under control? Is there enough light in winter?
- Is there enough possibility and space to move and play, do sports, make noise, etc.?
- Is there enough natural and green space, undefined space to explore? Will trees be planted in the streets?

The Ackermannbogen is mostly traffic free, so it can be considered healthy with respect at least to emissions and noise. The lighting was planned in accordance with prevailing rules and therefore should be sufficient. The amount of space for children's play and sports as well as green and undefined space can be considered large, at least in comparison with other city areas.

3. Usability

- Are spaces for children and youth close enough to their homes and reachable? Are they big enough?
- Are there unnecessary barriers?
- Is there shelter for bad weather or sunny days?
- Are there enough bike racks?
- Is there a possibility to linger or hang out?

As I've amply mentioned, Ackermannbogen arranged for continuity of space between houses and outdoors with few to no fences, so the play spaces are definitely reachable for children. There is little shelter from sun or bad weather, but the shipping container in the sports area has provided some remedy to that. It can be considered that there are too few spaces to linger and hang out and too few bike racks.

4. Flexibility

- Are there possibilities for children and youth to change their spaces according to their own needs and wishes?
- Are the planning instruments flexible enough to adapt to changing needs and demands by young users?
- Does the traffic concept allow temporary closure for traffic in favour of a use as play space?

These are partially true for Ackermannbogen. There are some possibilities to appropriate and change spaces according to children's needs and wishes, but compared with a designated nature playground or building playgrounds there is still little. As seen with the example of the shipping container, there is some flexibility in answering to changing needs and demands. Since there is already very little traffic, there is no need for closing it down in the area.

5. Participation

- Can children and youth participate in the planning? Are they informed appropriately and in time?
- Are institutions of children and youth care engaged in the planning process?
- Are the plannings understandable for children and youth?

Since the Ackermannbogen was a community project from the start, children's and families' needs and interests were implemented largely and timely in the planning. It is not possible, however, to evaluate the quality and quantity of children's direct participation in the process.

6. Experience and diversity

- Are public spaces lively and suitable for multiple uses by diverse groups (different ages, genders, cultures, abilities, etc.)?
- Do public spaces support the coexistence of different cultures?
- Are housing areas suitable for a diverse mix of residents?
- Do public playable spaces facilitate a variety of play experiences (adventure playgrounds, water play, meadows, hedges, bare lands, etc.)?

As I have outlined, there is rather high diversity among the residents at Ackermannbogen, and there are also frequent opportunities for them to meet and interact in public spaces. Furthermore, the outdoor spaces facilitate a variety of play experiences, although they could be more diverse.

By my measuring, Ackermannbogen fulfils many of the catalogue's criteria for a child-friendly neighbourhood as well as a host of the patterns linked to the development of social capital for child growth. The physical setting of the complex functionally supports the life of a community that has invisible meshes of human relations. Children's interests were considered from the beginning, and their needs therefore integrated in many ways. There are play territories according to different age groups and various institutions for child care in age-appropriate ranges.

The vast green areas at Ackermannbogen can serve as an alternative to screens and indoor activities, and playgrounds, the community gardens and the various events of Nachbarschaftshilfe are popular gathering spaces for families. The reduction in traffic and the designed-for-people public spaces invite street play and human interactions. Elements like these are often seen in research as important factors for building social capital. Collective and cooperative housing like in Ackermannbogen can thus be seen as an appropriate environment for building social capital for child growth.

7. Conclusions

The special physical and social elements of the Ackermannbogen encourage outdoor play and thus nurture their growth. The neighbourhood exemplifies how children can be accepted and respected in society and how their needs and wishes can be taken seriously in building and planning housing environments. Cooperative and collective housing environments bring people together and are therefore good learning environments for promoting and learning democratic and community values such as helping each other and knowing and respecting different age groups and cultures but also for finding one's own spaces for creativity and autonomy. Ackermannbogen is a good example of efforts to create a community where people can live together and practice community and face the challenges of our time. Easily accessible outdoor environments such as those at this project proved to be crucial during the COVID-19 pandemic lockdowns when it was mostly not possible to meet in person.

Lastly, vast outdoor spaces and connections to natural environments are an indispensable asset in preparing kids for future challenges like climate and environmental crises. In the right conditions and surroundings, with plenty of possibilities for contact and interaction, they will learn how to love and take responsibility for their fellow human beings and their natural environments.

The history of the Ackermannbogen housing complex shows that involving the actual future inhabitants in the planning process creates a much more human-centred living environment. There is much more space for people than for cars, traffic in general, or commerce in Ackermannbogen than in other neighbourhoods in Munich, and the community areas are well designed and in good use by people of all age groups. This chapter shows that Ackermannbogen is an ideal setting for children to develop rich social capital simply by their being exposed to community living in all its facets.

However, there are a few more factors that I did not consider here for children to really use the opportunities and possibilities that built living environments can provide. Factors like weather and climate, political atmosphere or a demanding and time-consuming school system could lead to kids spending less time outside, trusting other people less or simply having less time for leisure activities, but I did not consider these factors.

Additionally, the methods of this qualitative description are limited. The exact interactions of a cooperative housing environment such as Ackermannbogen and the development of social capital should be examined in more extensive, experimental research settings to validate any conclusions here.

Grant information

This work was supported by JSPS KAKENHI Grant Number JP20H02323.

References

Ackermannbogen eV. (2023). *Nachbarschaft Umwelt Kultur*. Ackermannbogen eV. https://ackermannbogen-ev.de/nachbarschaftsboerse/

Landeshauptstadt München. (2000). *Spielen in München. Bd. 3. Kriterienkatalog "Kinder- und Jugendfreundliches Planen"*. https://orlis.difu.de/handle/difu/279335

Stadt München. (2023). *Ackermannbogen*. Portal München Betriebs GmbH & Co. KG. https://stadt.muenchen.de/infos/ackermannbogen.html

wagnis eG. (2023). *Wohnbaugenossenschaft wagnis eG*. https://www.wagnis.org/

5
CHILD-REARING SOCIAL CAPITAL IN COLLECTIVE HOUSING IN JAPAN

Nobuko Matsumoto

1. Introduction: advantages of co-housing for families with young children

How children live and with whom they grow up have significant impacts on their mental and physical development. Their relationships with their family members and the spaces where they live are foundational for their healthy development.

Since the 1960s, the number of nuclear families has increased rapidly in Japan, and the average household size shrank from 3.97 in 1961 to 2.99 in 1992 and down to 2.27 in 2020. Households composed of parents and children accounted for 42.1% of all households in the 1980s, but this decreased to 25.0% by 2020. In contrast, the ratio of couple-only and single-person households accounted for 28.0%. Figure 5.1 graphically displays how household structures have changed over time in Japan.

Because the numbers of family members living together has decreased, family lifestyles involving children have undergone considerable changes; for instance, children now have fewer opportunities to interact across generations with their grandparents. With these changes, it became difficult for small households to perform tasks that used to be managed by family members living under the same roof, such as raising children and looking after the sick. Many roles that family members used to share have been moved to social or external domains, but not every responsibility can be externalised; some domestic work simply has to be managed by the people in the home. In particular, couples and single parents with young children face a wide variety of daily household tasks that are difficult for only the people living in the home to carry out, such as completing the daily housekeeping when

DOI: 10.4324/9781003456223-7

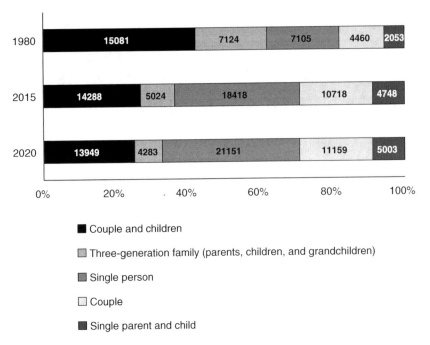

FIGURE 5.1 Changes in family structure.

someone is sick as well as tending to the sick and accompanying children to and from school. Managing such tasks poses enormous mental, physical, and economic burdens for people raising children in small households. This chapter focuses on collective houses, residential complexes for shared living where multiple families collaborate to share the housework that small households with children can have difficulty managing. I describe the advantages and potential of shared living for raising children.

2. The significance of collaborative living for families with young children

As mentioned, Sweden's collective houses enable collaborative living whereby families share their housework. They were introduced to Japan around 1990 (Koyabe & The Jusokenken Research Foundation Committee for Collective Housing, 2012), and Hyogo Prefectural Fureai Housing was built as a reconstruction of public housing for those affected by the Great Hanshin-Awaji Earthquake of 1995 (Ishito et al., 2000). The project started with six houses as Hyogo Prefecture Katayama Fureai Housing for August 1997 move-in, and 342 houses were eventually completed the housing in 10 places. These homes were built for the elderly victims of the disaster in the hope that they would help form mutually supportive relationships through interactions with each other and alleviate their isolation and loneliness. However, the elderly moved in without being fully aware of the philosophy of collective housing, and it was difficult for them to undertake residential management as voluntary collaborators because of their age.

The concept of collective houses in Sweden is said to have begun in the 1920s with the construction of an urban apartment complex where the residents jointly employed personnel in charge of housework (Thiberg, 1996). Formally, architect Sven Markelius (1889–1972) met social reformer Alva Raimer Myrdal in 1935 and built a collective house in Stockholm with his support. The collective house provided childcare facilities, communal kitchens, and meeting rooms, thus offering a new way of life for residents to live together and consolidate housework.

Although it was uncommon in the country and failed to gain social support, this form of housing (hotel apartments with housekeeping and childcare services and classic collectible houses) continued being built with support from some quarters. It attracted attention as a subject of study of the co-living model of housing in the 1970s, and the idea spread among European countries. Vestbro (1982) stated that many citizens misunderstood collective houses as being for privileged classes. This misunderstanding was because left-wing intellectuals led the movement for their construction, but their ideas were never part of the housing policy. However, he pointed out that the lack of support for collective housing was due to women's low influence on policy decisions and housing plans, which led to an absence of services for the residents (Mizumura, 2014).

More than 50 years after the study, Swedish women's involvement in policy making and planning has increased along with their social participation, and now, communal housing supply companies and construction unions have achieved results in building such houses; collective houses suitable for seniors or families with young children have been built. Furthermore, there are indications that people have started regarding collective housing as a more rewarding form of residence, as more houses have been constructed through resident participation. As of 2018, 58 cases had been built including during planning in Sweden (Ohashi et al., 2019). These findings suggest that the foundation is being laid to attract social support for the co-living model of housing.

According to Ikuko Koyabe (Ishito et al., 2000), who introduced collective houses to Japan, the basic concept of their self-work model can be summarised as follows:

- It is a private (exclusive) residential complex.
- It has communal spaces as an extension of a dwelling.
- It has living environments that provide social and mental independence and support through residents' proactive participation and collaboration in residential management.

- It is a form of living chosen by residents themselves.
- It is a form of residence available to men and women of all ages.

In short, a collective house is a residential complex with various shared spaces in addition to exclusive dwellings for individual households (e.g. shared kitchen, dining room, living room, laundry room, hobby room, terrace, garden, and storage) where residents live together and carry out housework collaboratively. They also discuss ways to use communal spaces as well as role sharing.

A lifestyle whereby residents support one another through proactive participation/collaboration in housing management is beneficial for families, particularly those raising children. For families with young children, the significance and advantages of the co-living model can be summarised as follows:

- It reduces the burden of housework and increases efficiency, creating free time and mental space for families raising children.
- Children have interactions with adults from diverse backgrounds while growing up. While many children raised in nuclear families only interact with a limited number of adults, co-living with numerous families enhances children's life experiences. Therefore, we can consider collective housing to be beneficial in gaining social capital.
- It also enables parents with young children to build relationships that provide them emotional support and for everyone to interact with diverse generations. Co-housing supports families in developing, becoming independent, and acquiring social capital.

Interviews conducted in 2021 with residents of collective housing who experienced the COVID-19 pandemic confirmed that having extra living space, including communal areas, and building relationships with multiple families based on collaboration made it possible to live without problem during the travel restrictions (Ohashi & Suzuki, 2021). They felt that the availability of common spaces and daily interactions with multiple families provided more emotional stability during the COVID-19 pandemic than living in a typical apartment complex (Ohashi & Suzuki, 2021). However, co-living also has the primary disadvantage that not all people will get along with each other. Some co-housing residents have reported stress related to role sharing in housework and interactions with fellow residents. People should be aware of this possibility before moving into collective housing.

3. Collective houses in Japan

The self-work model of collective houses was introduced to Japan in the early 1990s through a project initiated by Ikuko Koyabe and others; there are now at least six blocks of self-working collective houses within the private sector in Japan. Kankanmori, constructed in 2003, is Japan's first apartment complex operated and managed by its tenants (Morino Kaze Issue, 2014). It is located on the second and third floors of the Nippori Community in Nippori, Arakawa Ward (Figure 5.2) (Ishito et al., 2000).

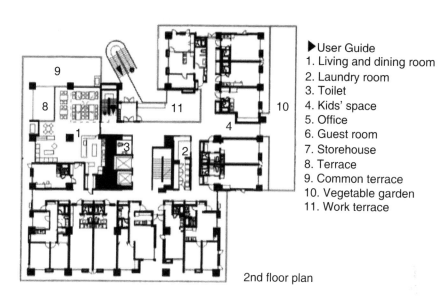

▶User Guide
1. Living and dining room
2. Laundry room
3. Toilet
4. Kids' space
5. Office
6. Guest room
7. Storehouse
8. Terrace
9. Common terrace
10. Vegetable garden
11. Work terrace

2nd floor plan

3rd floor plan

FIGURE 5.2 Floor plan of Japan's first collective house, Kankanmori.

Kankanmori is part of a 12-story, multigenerational community house built in 2003 on the former site of Nippori Junior High School. It is a multiple-facility complex with a nursery school, a medical clinic (1st floor); Collective House Kankanmori, rental housing for multiple generations including young people (2nd and 3rd floors); assisted living residence for the elderly (4th, 5th, and 6th floors); and homes for the elderly to live independently (7th–11th floor). It is collectively subleased to the residents' union that manages the housing and comprises 28 houses (24 m^2–62 m^2) with 166 m^2 of communal spaces including a kitchen and a dining room. Residents must participate in role sharing for at least one collaborative task (cleaning, cooking, equipment maintenance, public relations, gardening, etc.) and (around 10) group activities. On the second-floor terrace, the residents grow seasonal vegetables and flowers, making it a place where they can interact with others and children can feel the soil with their hands. Then at communal meals, residents of all ages living together can interact with one another through coworking and eating together.

Twenty years after it was built, the co-living building including Kankanmori still reflects the benefits of co-living. Today, the residents union still operates the housing complex, and the residents discuss issues such as dealing with aging residents and inviting and selecting new tenants in addition to the day-to-day management. For instance, aging residents necessitate changes in role sharing for housework as they become unable to labour. Some also consider the rent unaffordable, perhaps because they are not regular users of the communal spaces and facilities. The aging of the building and equipment over the years has also likely affected how the residents carry out their maintenance; they have gained and are gaining experience as they face challenges in managing the housing complex themselves.

As of 2022, as the numbers of single-person and couple-only households rise and there is a social mood to reconsider work–life balance, there is increased interest in building houses that offer such a residential model. In addition to collective houses, residential complexes for co-living are being built as shared houses and housing for the elderly, and support for this kind of housing as a new way of living is spreading.

4. Issues with collective houses in Japan

Japan does not have a large supply of collective houses. Although the advantage of a co-living housing model of has been recognised, the difficulty of constructing and maintaining them has been an obstacle to new supplies. There seem to be two main problems: there is a general negative perception among suppliers regarding the business profitability of collective houses, and people have negative attitudes towards co-living.

There is potential demand for co-housing models in Japan. In the past, many Japanese people sought their own wooden single-family homes as a life goal, and a large proportion of their assets comprised land and housing, but families raising children and elderly people who need support in daily life are looking for communal housing. The difference between the supply of collective houses between in Japan and Sweden is obvious, but the problem in Japan is that the supply is mostly provided by private companies, whereas it is mainly funded publicly in Sweden. It is difficult for suppliers to estimate demand, and they doubt it will be profitable. The construction of Collective House Kankanmori was a project to utilise the former site of a junior high school in Arakawa and can be considered an example of an experimental initiative.

Furthermore, the residents of collective houses participate in role-sharing as partners in collaborative living; if someone moves in without understanding this practice, it will cause confusion not only to the person but also to other residents. Even in Sweden, selecting tenants for collective housing is not easy. Some resident unions conduct the selection themselves because it would be tricky to maintain a communal life in housing that anyone could move into. With a publicly funded supply, the selection of tenants must be fair, which may discourage scrutinising potential residents to judge whether they can form collaborative relationships with others.

As for Collective House Kankanmori, the residents' union has a sublease agreement with the owner and continues to run communal living with the union members selecting tenants. However, in addition to managing communal life, they are responsible for vacant houses, which increases the union's economic burden. Furthermore, there are concerns that residents can feel burdened by the role-sharing responsibilities as they age and can perform less labour.

Notably, the Japanese people have diverse understandings of communal living, and the distances among residents affects the division of roles and responsibilities in collaboration, which can cause stress. Much of the potential demand for the co-housing is likely to come from residents who do not have a high level of functional independence, such as the elderly. These residents are likely to face difficulties in participation and collaboration, as in the case of Kobe City Reconstruction Public Housing. In response, it is essential to not only construct housing complexes based on the advantages of the co-living model of housing but also construct co-housing lifestyles that can be practiced in people's own separately built residences. We should build a system that allows people to live collectively by enjoying close relationships without living in a housing complex constructed as a collective house.

5. Conclusion

Collective houses are based on the philosophy of proactive participation and collaboration in residential management and provide living environments where residents build socially and mentally independent relationships of mutual support. Thus, those who live there should be able to build social capital throughout their daily lives. I argue that growing up in such an environment embodies how to build social capital. The co-living model of housing seems to be in demand for people who live independently to build new relationships in modern urban life, when intimate interactions among neighbours have become rare.

Grant information

This work was supported by JSPS KAKENHI Grant Number JP20H02323.

References

Ishito, I., & The Collective Support Group. (2000). *Collective housing in the middle of endeavor*. Gakugei Publishing.
Koyabe, I., & The Jusokenken Research Foundation Committee for Collective Housing. (2012). *The third housing: All about collective housing*. X-Knowledge.
Mizumura, H. (2014). *Sweden: Designing society for the housing for life*. Shokokusha.
Morino Kaze Issue. (2014). *This is a collective house!* Domesu Publishing.
Ohashi, S., Matsumoto, N., & Okazaki, A. (2019). *The supply system and operation of collective houses in Sweden*, Part 1–3. The Architecture Institute of Japan Conference.
Ohashi, S., & Suzuki, A. (2021). The actual situation of symbiotic housing under the influence of novel coronavirus infections: A survey of three cases of self-work collective houses. *The 73rd Annual Meeting of the Japan Society of Home Economics, 73*, 70.
Thiberg, S. (1996). *Housing research and design in Sweden*, (trans.into Japanese by T. Toyama). Kajima Publishing.
Vesbro, D. U. (1982). *Kollektivhus fran enkokshus till bogemenskap*. Stockholm. (Statens rad for byggnadsforskning T28).

PART III
Play spaces and the Bullerby model

6

CHILDREN'S PLANNED AND UNPLANNED PLACES OF PLAY AND ENCOUNTER IN WEST HERTTONIEMI, HELSINKI

Veera Moll and Eva Purkarthofer

1. Introduction

The built environment reflects ideologies about how children are expected to use cities and what characterises child-friendly cities and neighbourhoods. As cities grew and expanded in the 20th century, the numbers of sandboxes, swings, and slides increased. Built playgrounds became the most common way to include children's need for play in urban planning (Freeman, 2020). However, from the early stages, the creation of playgrounds and, more broadly, child-specific spaces – distinctive elements of modern childhood – drew criticism for isolating youth and redirecting children from lively streets to playgrounds (Jacobs, 1961; Zeiher, 2001). Urban geographer Lia Karsten has characterised playgrounds as spaces aimed at compensating for the daily restrictions children experience in urban environments (Karsten, 2003), whereas Kim Rasmussen uses the dichotomy *places for children*, referring to places created for children by adults, and *children's places*, describing places that children use and find meaningful, to conceptualise children's encounters with the environment. (Rasmussen, 2004).

The Bullerby model

To assess child friendliness in urban environments, Marketta Kyttä developed what she called the Bullerby model (Broberg et al., 2013/2006, Kyttä, 2003, 2004). It combines the degree of children's independent mobility with the number of children's actualised affordances in their environment, resulting in a two-by-two matrix with four types of environments (see Figure 6.1). According to Kyttä (2003), the ideal environment is characterised by high

DOI: 10.4324/9781003456223-9

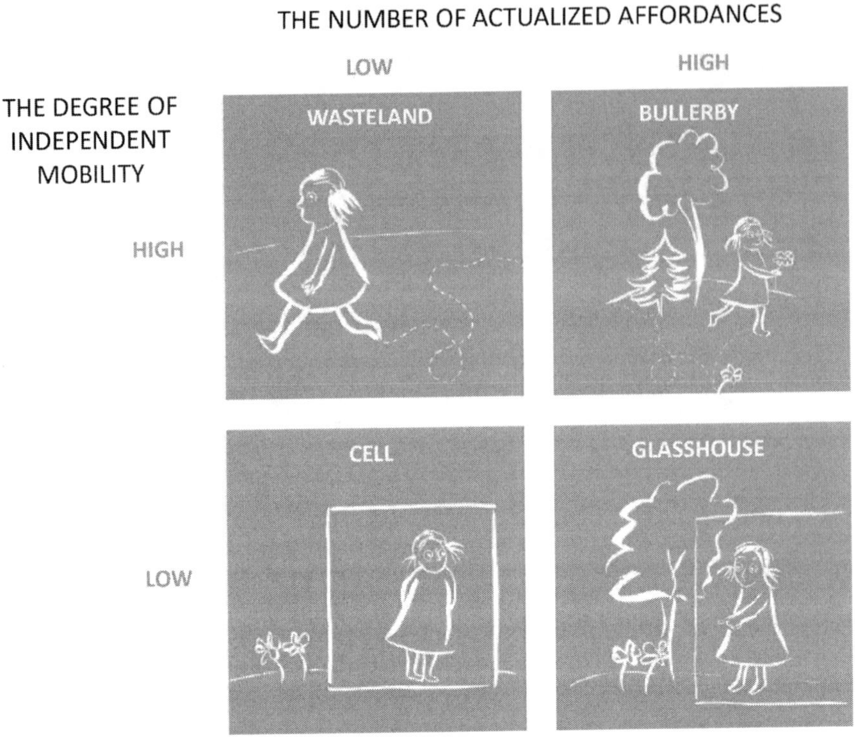

FIGURE 6.1 The Bullerby model.
Source: Marketta Kyttä.

independent mobility and a high number of actualised affordances. She named this scenario Bullerby, nodding to Astrid Lindgren's series of children's novels of the same name, which describe the life of a group of children in a Swedish village.

In Astrid Lindgren's Bullerby stories, children are part of everyday life and have a meaningful role in society, but above all, they have their own minds and a desire to explore, understand, and shape the world around them. The other types of environments are the *wasteland*, in which children can move independently but encounter a dull environment with few affordances; the *cell*, in which mobility is low and thus children cannot find affordances; and the *glasshouse*, where the environment offers high affordances, but children cannot experience them due to low independent mobility. In the Bullerby model, independent mobility and actualised affordances are not static values but are interdependent. For instance, low affordances in the cell scenario might decrease children's motivation to explore the environment, while in Bullerby, a positive interactive cycle can develop where actualised affordances motivate the child to move in the environment and as a result, new affordances become actualised (Kyttä, 2003, p. 98). The Bullerby model is useful for understanding that child friendliness is not limited to creating environments that appeal to children: children also need to be enabled to use these environments independently.

Research aims and methods

Inspired by Rasmussen's dichotomy and Kyttä's Bullerby model, in this chapter we investigate the roles of built play spaces and other places children use in the creation of a child-friendly environment in the suburban neighbourhood West Herttoniemi in Helsinki, Finland. West Herttoniemi was planned and built mainly in the 1950s and thus reflects the ideologies of planning at that time, which include certain conceptions about how children are supposed to move in and use the city. The neighbourhood thus provides interesting insights into the ascribed role of children in a city at a time of rapid urbanisation and increasing acknowledgement of children's needs.

While the spatial structure of West Herttoniemi is well preserved, we do not provide a historical analysis of the neighbourhood but aim to discuss the importance of planned and unplanned places of play for children today. We investigate the spatial distribution, character, and use of various types of built and natural environments by children to uncover the child friendliness of the neighbourhood and the underlying assumptions about child-friendly environments prevalent in Finland. In this chapter, we focus on toddlers and preschool children under the age of seven years, while discussing also some implications for older children and families as a whole.

Our analysis builds on two types of data. First, we mapped all planned places of play – namely different types of playgrounds – in West Herttoniemi in 2020. The mapping was carried out with Maptionnaire, a software application which combines spatially referenced GIS data and qualitative data. We classified the mapped playgrounds according to their size, function, and ownership (supervised city playgrounds, school and day care yards, small city playgrounds, and play areas in the yards owned by private housing companies). Additionally, we recorded the available playground equipment and took pictures of all playgrounds. Second, we observed and photographed the urban environments in West Herttoniemi between 2019 and 2022. The focus of this participatory observation was to understand how children and families use different parts of the neighbourhood.

Chapter structure

This chapter proceeds as follows: Section 2 elaborates on the spatial context and historical development of West Herttoniemi while also providing some insights into urban planning for children in Finland generally. Section 3 and Section 4 introduce the various planned and unplanned places of play in West Herttoniemi respectively. In Section 5, the results of the analysis are reviewed from the perspective of Rasmussen's dichotomy and Kyttä's Bullerby model. Section 6 discusses the findings with a view to recent developments related to early childhood education and care in Finland, social justice, and urban development proposals for the area. Section 7 concludes the chapter with a short summary.

2. Spatial context and history of West Herttoniemi

West Herttoniemi is a residential district in Helsinki, the capital of Finland. It is located approximately seven kilometres east of the city centre and is connected to the centre and to eastern Helsinki through the metro and an urban motorway (Figure 6.2). Large scale building began in the area in the 1950s during a time of urbanisation in Finland, when many dwellers from rural parts of the country moved to the bigger cities. At the same time, Finland experienced its first wave of suburbanization. Many families living in city centers moved away from their cramped housing conditions to newly built suburbs. As a result, cities expanded, and the first post-World War II suburban districts were built in Helsinki. West Herttoniemi thus is among the oldest post-war suburban neighbourhoods in Finland.

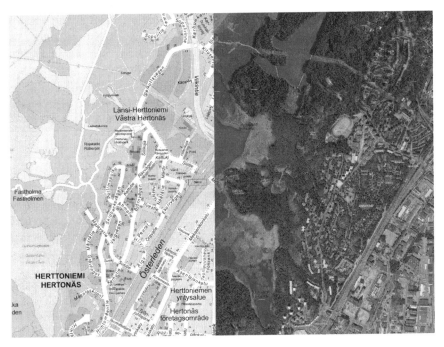

FIGURE 6.2 Guide map (left) and orthophotograph (right) of West Herttoniemi downloaded from Helsinki Map Service and reproduced under the license Creative Commons Attribution 4.0.

The area is characterised by four- to eight-storey apartment buildings which are loosely scattered among the hilly terrain and forestry landscape. The eastern part of the neighbourhood consists largely of row houses and detached houses which were built during the 1950s. Some newer blocks of flats were added in the southern and northern parts of the area during the 2010s and 2020s, respectively. The western part of the neighbourhood remained largely unbuilt and is designated as valuable nature area characterised by forest, the shore with its reed landscape, and significant differences in elevation, creating a cliff that delineates the residential area on top from the nature area at the bottom. In 2020, approximately 8,800 residents lived in West Herttoniemi, including 590 children under 7 and 617 children between 7 and 15 years old (Helsinki Region Infoshare, 2023).

Families with children were at the core of suburban planning in 1950s Finland. The intimate forest suburb scale with buildings and roads following the shapes of the terrain offered an abundance of built and unbuilt places for play (Saarikangas et al., 2023). Relatively moderate amounts of motorised traffic as well as the high number of children further increased the child friendliness of the suburbs. Depictions of suburban life in the 1950s resemble today's situation in many ways, although there are fewer children and more cars. West Herttoniemi is still very popular among families, and the demand especially for bigger family apartments is higher than the supply.

3. Planned places of play

In this section, we describe different planned places of play in Herttoniemi, which according to Rasmussen (2004) can be classified as places for children since they were intentionally created by adults to be used by children.

There are two playgrounds (*leikkipuisto* in Finnish) in West Herttoniemi that are run by the city of Helsinki (Figure 6.3). The outdoor parts of these playgrounds are open all year round and are accessible 24/7. The playgrounds have various types of equipment such as sandboxes, swings, slides, a carousel, a seesaw, trampolines, balance boards, and in some cases unheated swimming pools. Typically, a part of the playground targeted at smaller children is fenced in, while there is also some play equipment, especially for older kids, outside the fenced area and some possibilities for play in the surrounding meadows and forests.

Additionally, the playgrounds have indoor premises which are open on weekdays during working hours. During these hours, playground supervisors who are employed by the city are present and organise various free activities in the playgrounds. These activities can take place indoors or outdoors and are intended for children together with their parents; that is, playground staff are not liable for children participating in these activities. Examples for activities include music and singing, baby group, and various sports and games.

FIGURE 6.3 View to the fenced area and indoor premises of the city-run playground Squirrel Park (Leikkipuisto Orava). Photograph by Veera Moll.

While staff are present, children can also use tricycles, sports equipment, and sandbox toys that belong to the playground. During the summer school holidays, the city of Helsinki also offers free soup lunch for children under 16 years. This tradition was established in the 1940s and has remained almost unchanged ever since. No pre-registration is required to use the free lunch offer, but children are expected to bring their own plate and cutlery to reduce waste and costs. The lunch offered by the city aims to make everyday life easier for families and to ensure that children in Helsinki get at least one warm meal per day – which they would usually get in their childcare institution or school – also during the holidays.

Parents can also choose to sign up their school-aged children for an after-school club at the city-run playgrounds. In these clubs, children receive a snack and can participate in activities organised by the staff; they can also play freely or use the time to do their homework. During these afternoon hours, children are supervised by playground staff from the city, and participation is subject to a small fee.

In addition, there are six smaller *leikkipaikka* in West Herttoniemi. These play spaces are owned by the city and they can be used all year around and the whole day. However, they have no indoor areas, no facilities like toilets, and no organised activities with staff. Their play equipment typically includes swings, slides, sandbox, and rockers, with some variation. Most of these play spaces are not fenced in, and therefore, the natural formations and surroundings might create distinctive features which children incorporate in their play.

There are also three schools and two public kindergartens located in West Herttoniemi; their playgrounds are primarily used by the children who attend these institutions during working hours. However, the playgrounds are never locked off and can be used outside the school hours and on the weekends by everyone. They are especially popular in the evenings and weekends, as they offer simple sports facilities for school-aged kids which differ from the typical playground equipment.

Moreover, there is a city-owned sports fields in West Herttoniemi which includes a football field, running tracks and tennis courts. In the winter, an ice-skating rink is maintained on the sports field. The sports field is used by adults and children alike, and various events are organised there.

Additionally, there are numerous play areas in private yards. It was not until 1973 that the first legislative requirements were established, according to which adequate space for playgrounds also had to be allocated within the lots of apartment buildings. The new requirements did not directly concern the already built yards, but the public and professional discussions on play spaces, the increasing number of recommendations preceding and following the statute, and the play space and play equipment standardisation, as well as the growing play equipment industry, increased the number of play areas all over the city (Moll & Jouhki, 2021). The apartment building play areas vary in size and equipment, but due to the equipment standardisation and the few companies ruling the play equipment market, the play spaces look rather similar. Typical play equipment includes sandbox, rocker, swings, and slides. In our mapping, we identified close to 70 private yard play areas in West Herttoniemi which are distributed relatively evenly across the neighbourhood. Figure 6.4 shows an example.

4. Play beyond assigned boundaries

In this section, we describe different places that are not specifically dedicated to children but that they nonetheless use to play, bearing some similarities to Rasmussen's concept of children's places. The discussion of these unplanned places of play is based on our observations of children's use of space in West Herttoniemi. We cannot claim that the descriptions of these areas are comprehensive, as they are characterised by their unbound nature and cannot be easily delineated. Nevertheless, this section serves to illustrate how the environment can cater to children's needs even when this is not the explicit intention.

FIGURE 6.4   Private yard play area and surroundings. Photograph by Veera Moll.

The streets in West Herttoniemi are not play areas per se, but the moderate traffic and the culture of children's independent mobility in Finland enable children to occasionally play in the streets. With the urban motorway bordering the neighbourhood to the east, the area itself has less through traffic. Figure 6.5 displays the newly completed shared bike path and sidewalk.

Many natural features in the neighbourhood offer affordances for children. West Herttoniemi is built on hilly terrain, and the geological formations such as big boulders and small cliffs invite play. The residential apartment buildings are built on or alongside these natural features, and thus the transitions from built to unbuilt areas are smooth.

Forest areas are located mostly on the western side of the neighbourhood, although smaller groups of trees can be found all over the area. In addition, bushes and shrubs grow alongside streets and between buildings. Forests and bushes offer opportunities for kids to play with tree branches, build huts, or collect leaves and pinecones.

Moreover, berries such as raspberries, wild strawberries, and bilberries grow in these forests and can be picked by anyone under Finland's everyman's right. These activities hold the potential to enhance children's engagement with nature. The shore marks the western boundary of the neighbourhood. While the sea is not immediately accessible (there are no beaches in the area), children can explore the rocks and reed landscape (Figure 6.6).

Children's planned and unplanned places of play in Helsinki 95

FIGURE 6.5   Shared bike path and sidewalk in West Herttoniemi. Photograph by Veera Moll.

FIGURE 6.6   Natural rock formation creating affordances for children. Photograph by Veera Moll.

A more defining characteristic of the neighbourhood than the natural features per se is the fact that extensive nature strips exist between residential buildings. There is no fencing towards nature or between apartment buildings which creates a largely barrier-free environment which offers a variety of affordances for children.

5. Looking for Bullerby in West Herttoniemi

The previous sections have introduced the various planned and unplanned places of play in West Herttoniemi. A distinction between planned and unplanned is useful for drawing attention to the fact that children do not only play in the areas designed for them. However, it is also challenging to draw a clear line between the two categories since planned and unplanned places sometimes seamlessly connect, as can be seen for example in the play areas located in private yards. The physical environment surrounding these play areas often is equally (or more) enticing for children to explore as the play area furniture itself.

Generally, the number of planned places of play is very high in West Herttoniemi, comprising both city-run public playgrounds and play areas in private yards which are accessed by the residents of a specific building but also other families living close by. While private in legal terms, these play areas are thus not closed off or exclusive to residents in practice. The high number and sometimes rather uninspired design of private play areas raises the question whether these places follow the principle of quantity over quality. Potentially, more enticing and varied play areas could be created by bundling resources from various apartment houses rather than building a small and standardised play area for each building.

However, the high number of planned play areas serves as clear indication that children have their place in the (sub)urban environment, and the dense network of planned places of play makes children visible and welcome in the neighbourhood. The city-run playgrounds, including their activities, afternoon program and free lunch during the school holidays, offer another layer of engagement for children in the area. In West Herttoniemi, and Helsinki in general, it is therefore a combination of spatial and social features that contributes to the child-friendly environment.

Often, children do not hesitate to expand their play beyond the planned play areas and use natural formations and features to create different places of play, even when playground equipment is standardised. In one yard, a set of sandbox and swing might thus be interesting because it is located next to a couple of rocks which can be climbed, and in another yard, there might be forest and brush to explore next to swing and sandbox, thus creating a different experience for the children. Unplanned places of play also change drastically with the changing nature and different seasons throughout the year. Fallen autumn leaves, rain puddles, snow, or high grass are just some of

FIGURE 6.7 Private yard in wintertime with sandbox hidden under the snow. Photograph by Veera Moll.

the seasonal features that offer interesting possibilities and experiences for children. However, especially for toddlers, seasonal changes to the environment such as ice and snow might also significantly limit their mobility, and playground equipment might become unserviceable due to large quantities of snow. Additionally, a lack of natural light during the wintertime and insufficient artificial lighting makes the use of both planned and unplanned places of play challenging (Figure 6.7).

Our analysis confirms that West Herttoniemi can be understood as urban environment which enables children to experience a high number of actualised affordances through a high degree of independent mobility, and therefore it could be considered a Bullerby environment (Kyttä, 2003). The spatial structure of the neighbourhood is a main factor contributing to this assessment. The yards between buildings, although privately owned, are often open and accessible, and there is no fencing between buildings or between residential areas and nature areas such as forests. This enables kids to explore the surroundings of their home. The nature strips between buildings offer plenty of affordances for kids of different ages.

The network of small play areas as part of residential yards offers close-by opportunities for play, especially for younger kids. Additionally, these play areas hold the potential for children and parents to get to know their neighbours and thus contribute to enhancing the social life – and social capital – among families in the area.

The affordances in the original Bullerby model by Kyttä (2003) were predominantly functional affordances and included only a few affordances for sociality. That is, the social dimension of actualising affordances was not the focus of the Bullerby model. In reality, typically almost all actualisations of affordances include social and emotional aspects and thus can enhance bonding (within groups) and bridging (between groups) social capital (Lancee, 2010). Our analysis suggests that the presence and visibility of children in the city, often especially tangible around planned places of play, motivates more families to spend time outdoors. However, the social aspects of environmental child friendliness deserve a closer look in the future.

While the Bullerby model builds on the idea of children's independent mobility, we have to acknowledge that children younger than seven years, who were our focus in this chapter, typically do not move around neighbourhoods independently. However, even if parents are participating in the play of such younger children, children's agency and ability to explore the environment can be considered age-appropriate independent mobility. Learning to have agency in their environments early on can enhance children's ability to move and explore independently when older.

6. Discussion

Our study shows that West Herttoniemi can be considered a child-friendly environment in many respects. A dense network of playgrounds maintained by the city as well as numerous play areas in private yards contribute to the perceived presence of children in the neighbourhood and offer opportunities for play close to home. In addition to these planned places of play, the natural environment and spatial structure of West Herttoniemi create opportunities for play beyond these designated places for children. Such play beyond playgrounds enhances children's contact with nature and can bring essential benefits for children's health and well-being (Chawla, 2015).

Our analysis builds on mapping planned places of play and participatory observation to explore how children use the suburban environment for play. While these two research methods enable us to better understand children's needs and behaviour, we also acknowledge certain limitations to our approach. While we were able to systematically map the planned places of play, we did not comprehensively locate and collect all unplanned places of play.

Moreover, because we focussed on planned play places, our analysis is most accurate for younger children, approximately up to seven years, as older children often do not use these areas. Most importantly, however, as our analysis sets out from the built environment rather than from the residents of the area, we do not have any information on the children who do not spend time outdoors in the neighbourhood. In other words, we do not know whether some children use facilities in other neighbourhoods, spend time mostly in organised leisure activities (e.g. sports clubs), or do not spend time outdoors at all.

We also want to reflect critically on the recent developments related to early childhood education and urban planning in Finland generally and Helsinki specifically. First, many of the supervised playgrounds have been occasionally closed due to staff shortages in other city organisations, resulting for example in reassignments of playground supervisors to kindergartens. Even if a break in the playground service is only temporary, such phases might reduce the reliability of the service in the long run. Another challenge related to the supervised playgrounds is the lack of knowledge about the services among some families. In other words, some families are excluded from the service simply because they don't know about it (City of Helsinki, n.d.).

Second, as the city of Helsinki continues to attract residents and aims to provide new areas for residential development, a planning process to build more apartment blocks in West Herttoniemi is ongoing. While the suggestions for urban infill are relatively moderate and would not significantly alter the character of the neighbourhood in its entirety, they are questionable from the perspective of children's use of the environment. Specifically, some new buildings are being suggested in a small bog and woodland area and on a meadow next to one playground, both of which areas can clearly be identified as places that hold ample opportunities for children's play beyond assigned play spaces.

A first citizen participation event related to the plan proposal has highlighted that residents are sceptical of the infill proposal, especially in the area that is considered crucial for children's play. While we are appreciative of the idea of creating more apartments in a child-friendly and sought-after neighbourhood such as West Herttoniemi, it will be crucial to also acknowledge children's places in planning and not assume that the construction of dedicated playgrounds is sufficient to fulfil children's needs in the city. Comprehensive mapping of children's behavioural patterns as well as involvement of children in participatory planning processes can generate better knowledge of children's meaningful places (Björklid & Nordström, 2007; Kyttä et al., 2012).

Third, children's independent mobility is decreasing globally, and Finland is no exception to this trend, although by international comparison, Finnish children still move relatively independently (Kyttä et al., 2015). While in this chapter we investigated the built environment rather than tracing the movement of children in the area, we assume that moving freely (while not necessarily unsupervised) is essential for building lasting relationships with the environment. This is in line with Kyttä's Bullerby model through which she explains the interactive cycle between having agency over where to go and the actual affordances that can be experienced in a specific environment. If families use walking and biking as modes of transport, this involves children into moving actively in the city rather than making them passive passengers in the backseat of a car. At the same time, these active modes of transport allow smaller children to gain better knowledge about their built and natural environments, thus helping them to more easily navigate in the city.

7. Conclusion

In this chapter, we have discussed places for children and children's places (cf. Rasmussen, 2004) in West Herttoniemi, a suburban neighbourhood in Helsinki, Finland. Contextualising the neighbourhood according to Kyttä's (2003) Bullerby model, we conclude that West Herttoniemi can be considered child friendly in many respects due to the extensive network of city-run playgrounds and private play areas, as well as the natural environment that offers interesting and varied places for children to explore. The principles of planning with children's and families' needs in mind, prevalent during the first wave of suburbanisation in Helsinki in the 1950s, still shapes life in West Herttoniemi today.

The case of West Herttoniemi highlights that both planned and unplanned places of play are necessary for creating child-friendly urban environments. The dense network of private play areas, while sometimes perceived as simple and a little dull due to their standardised design, nonetheless encourages families to spend time outdoors, especially during the summer months. While designed for smaller kids, these play areas are crucial for parents too, as they create a sense of belonging among the residents in the area and thus enhance social capital. However, their use during winter is challenging due to harsh weather conditions, lack of sunlight, and inadequate illumination. Future developments, both in West Herttoniemi and elsewhere, should also acknowledge the existence and importance of unplanned play environments for children, which often run the danger of being unnoticed when urban developments are being proposed but are essential for enabling children's contact with the environment.

Grant information

This work was supported by JSPS KAKENHI Grant Number JP20H02323.

References

Björklid, P., & Nordström, M. (2007). Environmental child-friendliness: Collaboration and future research.*Children, Youth and Environments*, 17(4), 388–401.

Broberg, A., Kyttä, M., & Fagerholm, N. (2013). Child-friendly urban structures: Bullerby revisited. *Journal of Environmental Psychology*, 35, 110–120. https://doi.org/10.1016/j.jenvp.2013.06.001 (Original work published 2006, February)

City of Helsinki. (n.d.). *Kaikkien yhteinen, vetovoimainen leikkipuisto. Ohjeistus vetovoimaisten leikkipuistojen suunnitteluun.* Retrieved February 17, 2023, from https://www.hel.fi/static/liitteet/kaupunkiymparisto/julkaisut/ohjeet/Ohjeistus-vetovoimaisten-leikkipuistojen-suunnitteluun.pdf

Chawla, L. (2015). Benefits of nature contact for children. *Journal of Planning Literature, 30*(4), 433–452. https://doi.org/10.1177/0885412215595441

Freeman, C. (2020). Twenty-five years of children's geographies: A planner's perspective. *Children's Geographies, 18*(1), 110–121. https://doi.org/10.1080/14733285.2019.1598547

Helsinki Region Infoshare. (2023). *Helsinki: Population.* Retrieved February 17, 2023, from https://hri.fi/data/en_GB/dataset/helsinki-vaesto

Jacobs, J. (1961). *The death and life of great American cities.* Random House.

Karsten, L. (2003). Children's use of public space: The gendered world of the playground. *Childhood, 10*(4), 457–473. https://doi.org/10.1177/0907568203104005

Kyttä, A. M., Broberg, A. K., & Kahila, M. H. (2012). Urban environment and children's active lifestyle: Softgis revealing children's behavioral patterns and meaningful places. *American Journal of Health Promotion, 26*(5), 137–149. https://doi.org/10.4278/ajhp.100914-QUAN-310

Kyttä, M. (2003). *Children in outdoor contexts. Affordances and independent mobility in the assessment of environmental child friendliness.* Helsinki University of Technology.

Kyttä, M. (2004). *Ihmisystävällinen elinympäristö: Tutkimustietoa ja käytännön ideoita rakennetun ympäristön suunnittelua varten [Human-friendly environment: Research knowledge and practical ideas for urban planning and design].* YIT; Teknillinen korkeakoulu.

Kyttä, M., Hirvonen, J., Rudner, J., Pirjola, I., & Laatikainen, T. (2015). The last free-range children? Children's independent mobility in Finland in the 1990s and 2010s. *Journal of Transport Geography, 47*, 1–12. https://doi.org/10.1016/j.jtrangeo.2015.07.004

Lancee, B. (2010). The economic returns of immigrants' bonding and bridging social capital: The case of the Netherlands. *International Migration Review, 44*, 202–226, 84.

Moll, V., & Jouhki, E. (2021). Leikin paikka: Rakennettujen leikkiympäristöjen kehitys 1970-luvun Helsingissä. *Yhdyskuntasuunnittelu, 59*(1), 10–32. https://doi.org/10.33357/ys.99337

Rasmussen, K. (2004). Places for children – children's places. *Childhood, 11*(2), 155–173. https://doi.org/10.1177/0907568204043053

Saarikangas, K., Moll, V., & Hannikainen, M. (2023). Lived, material and planned welfare: Mass-produced suburbanity in 1960s and 1970s metropolitan Finland. In *Experiencing society and the lived welfare state.* Palgrave Macmillian.

Zeiher, H. (2001). Children's Islands in space and time: The impact of spatial differentation on children's ways of shaping social life. In M. du Bois-Raymond, H. Sünker, & H. H. Krüger (Eds.), *Childhood in Europe: Approaches–trends–findings.* Peter Lang.

7
BULLERBY AND THE VALUE OF PHYSICAL ENVIRONMENTS FOR SOCIAL CAPITAL

A Swedish example in times of change

Märit Jansson

1. Introduction

In this chapter, I present a small Swedish town and its qualities and challenges for children's social capital. It is an example of how the built environment can support child friendliness but also of how the child friendliness is dependent on various places and processes over time. To build and develop social capital and children's possibilities for outdoor play and independent mobility, child-friendly qualities cannot be taken for granted but need continuous attention by multiple actors. This includes in planning, design, and management for open spaces and independent mobility but also includes many different actors who can support, for example, social connection, freedom, and involvement (Jansson et al., 2022).

The concept of Bullerby

The books by Astrid Lindgren about children in the Bullerby are highly loved in Sweden, where *buller* means 'noise' and Bullerbyn 'the noisy village'; however, this is not purely negative but also gives an image of a lively environment. Lindgren's descriptions are much inspired by her own childhood in the 1920s and give a historical and to some extent idealised view of children's lives in a small rural village one hundred years ago. However, Kyttä's (2004) use of the concept of Bullerby to describe contemporary child-friendly environments where children have both independent mobility and affordances provides a new dimension, pointing out how relationships, both between people and with the landscape, affect children's places and independent mobility. This shows the importance of strong social capital for child friendliness.

DOI: 10.4324/9781003456223-10

Developing child-friendly environments in Sweden

The understanding of social capital in Swedish built environments today will have to take on historical perspectives also for reasons other than the rural 1920s Bullerby image and heritage. Sweden has a history of being attentive to the needs of children, including in urban planning, particularly during the mid-20th century. Early influences from England and Germany concerning outdoor environments for children and several influential voices among practitioners and associations led to the introduction of playgrounds and other adaptations from the late 19th century and in housing areas from the early 20th century (Nolin, 2016). The awareness and focus on children was demonstrated in play parks, play sculptures, and adventure playgrounds as well as at a UN conference on children's play spaces held in Stockholm, Sweden's capital, in 1958 (Nolin, 2016).

What Pries and Qviström (2021) among others describe as a welfare landscape was developed over several decades, most notably as a complex welfare discourse that materialised through planning for the Million Homes Programme in the 1960s and 1970s (Pries & Qviström, 2021). This included focus on leisure and recreation for public health and safeguarding spaces for children and others as well as a traffic planning, often to separate car traffic from pedestrians (Pries & Qviström, 2021). This modernist development has been criticised, including for the lack of variation in playgrounds, but it has provided valuable basic structures and facilities for child-friendly environments in Sweden up to today (Jansson & Persson, 2010).

During the last decades, planning ideals in Sweden have been highly affected by the densification discourse, often leading to major transformations of the landscapes from the welfare era (Qviström, 2022). Green and open spaces are often being used for urban development, justified by the request for urban growth, claiming open space quality rather than quantity, which demonstrates a shift in attitudes within planning (Littke, 2015). In parallel to this, the focus on children in particular in planning practice in the Nordic countries has also been decreasing for decades (Wilhjelm, 2002). This has led to large local differences in the child friendliness of environments throughout municipalities and neighbourhoods as new developments are made as infill in existing built areas. Research has thus called for more understanding of the assets of welfare planning before they become too transformed (Qviström, 2022).

Child-friendly environments and social capital

The child friendliness of an environment builds upon a complex web of various socio-physical qualities, as physical and social environments are highly interconnected (Kreutz, 2014; Jansson et al., 2022). Notably, Kyttä (2004) lifted the importance of children's independent mobility combined with a multitude of actualised affordances in the environment for supporting their use of outdoor environments for play etc. High levels of both these factors is a sign of the ideal child-friendly Bullerby. The combination of the social and physical also becomes clear in Wales et al.'s (2021) description of the connection between children's independent mobility and their agency connected to building a sense of community, where mobility and agency in children's local environments are interconnected.

It is argued that social capital in relation to children has not been sufficiently defined as a concept. Morrow (1999) suggested viewing it as mainly processes and practices that can lead to 'capital'. While this may be true, it is in the socio-physical environments that social capital is built and can be studied and understood. There is a need for various processes and actors to build child friendliness over time, where social capital can be a useful focus.

Children as catalysts of social capital

Social capital as connected to sense of community is a requirement for children's outdoor play and independent mobility, providing children with opportunities to develop relationships to both their local communities and their neighbourhoods at large, as well as to their peers (Pacilli et al., 2013). Such developments are positive both for children as individuals and for their communities.

For children, using and moving in local environments is connected to their physical activity (Stone et al., 2014) but also to a multitude of benefits including psycho-social, cognitive, and social competence; mental health; happiness; and sense of community (Marzi & Reimes, 2018). At community level, children can be actors and even agents of change (Malone, 2013); they have been described as catalysts of social capital, important for how social capital is both created and maintained locally, as connected to community participation and neighbourhood cohesion among families (Wood et al., 2013.) This includes children affecting how community social well-being is being built (Pacilli et al., 2013, p. 389). However, the last decades have included loss of social capital that contributes to parental safety concerns limiting the independent mobility of young people (Porskamp et al., 2019).

The supportive role of adults

On the social side, the adult world plays a paramount role in building social capital that supports children's outdoor use of spaces for play as well as other activities. A retrospective study of young adults' childhoods in a Canadian city revealed the importance of adults in building a sense of community in neighbourhoods to foster outdoor play (Holt et al., 2015). Holt et al. (2015) used the concept of 'the eyes on the street' (Jacobs, 1961), which points at the role of adults in facilitating children's active free play.

One aspect of this is adults' role in supporting children's independent mobility. This is heavily affected by how parents perceive the local physical and social environments (Pacilli et al., 2013; Veitch et al., 2017) and whether they find independent mobility valuable for their children, something that can be supported by proximity to green areas and by sense of community (Prezza et al., 2005). Children themselves can be part of building social capital locally when given the chance in supportive socio-physical contexts (Wales et al., 2021).

The role of physical environments in forming social capital

The physical environment and its development are also main influences on the processes taking place there, including building social capital, for both adults and children. Eriksson and Dahlblom (2020) found children's access to local, health-promoting places as related to social capital, where physical and social environments are interconnected. Mullenbach et al. (2022) describe equity in the quality of parks and neighbourhood environments as important for increasing social capital for families. Various ages can be included in open spaces that provide for well-balanced multi-functionality (Sundevall & Jansson, 2020), where for children their play, socialisation, and transport in the environment are often intertwined (Johansson et al., 2020).

Still, there is a lack of physical environmental focus in later studies of children and social capital. To better understand the possibilities and challenges connected to social capital as a corner stone for child-friendly environments, it is of value to provide case studies that describe how social capital can be built, or diminished, in various socio-physical contexts.

2. The example case and approach

The small town constituting the case has around 6,000 inhabitants, a number that is growing with increased housing construction. It is situated in southern Sweden, by the railway in between quite large cities and with other towns close. The built environment is a clear heritage from the welfare era, as large parts of the small town were planned during the 1960s, with mainly detached houses and some multifamily housing, schools and green spaces placed centrally, and a traffic plan limiting car access with a network of bicycle and walking paths. In recent years, new planning has heavily affected the area, first in the 1990s when more housing was built and more lately through both infill projects and urban sprawl, which has increased car access and traffic.

With both a varied provision of actualised affordances and comparably high independent mobility among children, the small town might be described as a Bullerby (Kyttä, 2004). A number of scholars have studied its environments and child friendliness, including Johansson et al. (2011), who found that children there had much more independent mobility than in other areas in the same municipality. They also found high levels of everyday physical activity, frequent play and socialisation with friends, and, among adults, a high sense of community (Johansson et al., 2011). Furthermore, Jansson et al. (2016) highlighted the value of traffic separation and the provision of varied spaces including with varied management levels, and Wales et al. (2021) emphasised the importance of children's agency and sense of community for locally developing independent mobility.

Jansson et al. (2016) and Wales et al. (2021) both build upon walking interviews in the form of child-led walks conducted in 2014 with children aged 10–11. At that age, children in Sweden and other Nordic countries tend to have sufficient independent mobility to move around in their neighbourhoods unaccompanied by adults (Björklid & Gummesson, 2013). During the child-led walks, the children themselves decided on where to go and which places to show, walking in groups of three or four peers for around two hours (Jansson et al., 2016). A new round of child-led walks with children the same age was conducted five years later, in 2019 (Jansson & Sunding, 2024). This repeated data collection has allowed for following up on the effects for children of the various plans that have been realised. This chapter is a reflection based on both these studies, as well as of my own impressions and experiences from the small town and its recent development.

3. Findings

Various places and affordances

A variety of places and the affordances found there appear to be a main asset for children's outdoor lives as well as for social capital in the small town, used among children, families, and others. In 2014, formal places such as playgrounds and green spaces, and informal places such as abandoned or unmanaged ones were identified during the child-led walks (Figure 7.1a), while in 2019, the children showed fewer abandoned places and more sport facilities and urban spaces (Figure 7.1b). This shows a turn towards more paved, designed, and formal places, following the loss of other types of places.

Local playgrounds have many functions, including as meeting places for families of younger children and also for older children and their peers who use them as meeting places as well as places for playing and socialising in their own age group (see Figure 7.2). Socialisation between children and adults has been mostly visible in playground settings and other park spaces with many affordances within the small town, as that is where families tend to gather. However, the children aged 10–11 also described that they had found their own playgrounds for themselves and their peers to meet and playing together, as they also like getting away from the families and small children in some of the playgrounds.

Neighbourhoods with special qualities for social capital

Some local neighbourhoods appear to particularly support the use of outdoor environments for children and others, functioning as intergenerational meeting places. These have in common that they have traffic solutions limiting car traffic and that there are spaces with various affordances available. Some of them are used mainly by those who live in the area, but there are also a few more dynamic examples of more variation in the environment and multiple functions.

One of them is around the local lower secondary school, where there are nearby detached housing, a library, sports facilities (an indoor sports hall but also outdoor ping-pong table, skateboard ramps, and a multisport court), green spaces (lawns, some shrubs and trees, a small public garden with a fountain, a storm water pond), and paved spaces. This forms a varied and

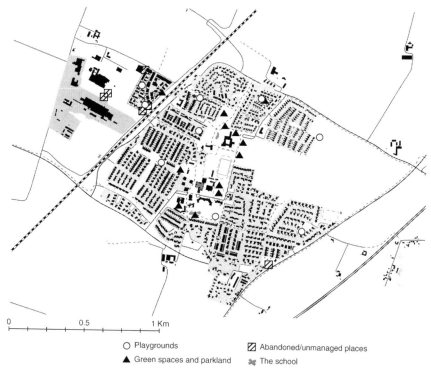

FIGURE 7.1   The places visited during the child-led walks in 2014 (a) and 2019 (b) were somewhat different, where the 2014 walks included more informal and abandoned places and the 2019 more formal places such as paved and sport areas. Maps by Mark Wales and Anna Sunding.

108 Märit Jansson

- ○ Playgrounds
- ⬢ Sport facilities
- ● Urban spaces
- ▲ Green spaces and parkland
- ▨ Abandoned/unmanaged places
- ✼ The school

FIGURE 7.1 (Continued)

FIGURE 7.2 Some of the local playgrounds are more used by families with small children, while others are more popular among older children who wish to meet with peers without being disturbed by other age groups. Photo by the author.

FIGURE 7.3   Multiple uses of the space around the lower secondary school by various age groups. Collage based on Google Maps and photos by the author.

walkable local environment (see Figure 7.3). It is used both by those living in the closest local neighbourhood and by others in the small town. This is an example of tessellated multifunction, where several different functions are placed next to each other (Sundevall & Jansson, 2020). Yet, there are some overlaps of functions and there are also uses drawing much attention to them, such as activities on the multisport court and skateboard ramps. Lately, however, development projects have also started to affect this area: the multisport court has been removed to make room for parking in the development of new buildings.

Temporal changes

Swedes do not always converse easily, even with their close neighbours in everyday settings, let along with complete strangers. However, some temporal changes facilitate social interaction, such as weather events, seasonal changes, and festivities. For example, at times when the local dams in a park developed during the last years freeze, ice skating becomes possible for a few days, and this creates a somewhat different social climate as well (see Figure 7.4). Local people of all ages gather around the ponds, drinking hot chocolate and chatting with other residents, all with focus on supporting the possibilities for children and youth in the area to have fun together and test some ice skating.

FIGURE 7.4   A frozen pond allowed ice skating for a few days, bringing residents together and building local social capital with the children in focus. Photo by the author.

Another temporary change, but one with possible long-term effects, was the COVID-19 pandemic. In Sweden, there were few restrictions, and none hindered people from going outdoors, so the use of outdoor environments in general increased during the pandemic, creating more possibilities for social interactions in local environments. This included organising parties and picnics in parks and nature areas but also more spontaneous uses around the small town, even communication (Figure 7.5). In this way, the pandemic might actually have had a positive effect on social capital in some areas in Sweden.

Changes with densification and more

During the child-led walks both in 2014 and 2019, the children brought up the development projects going on in the small town as a recurring theme. They felt that the changes in their local environment were happening fast, were difficult to follow, and were not taking their needs and perspectives into account. Some children had approached the local government about this but did not feel valued. During the walks, the children brought up the loss of spaces that they used to appreciate, such as an informal biking track that was organised by young locals on park land but removed for an infill project.

FIGURE 7.5 A message written on the tarmac of a local walking path saying 'Hi, I hope that you are fine' during the pandemic. Photo by the author.

The small town is clearly in a state of continuous and quite permanent change given that for several years, construction sites of various sizes and new structures have been appearing, affecting the lives of local children. The major change is that children are going from finding their own informal places to being steered to more formal spaces, including in a new rather large park.

In spring 2016, I gave a lecture at the local library, presenting and discussing child-friendly environments both in general and in the small town more specifically. One thing I particularly recall from that occasion was that persons attending the lecture told me about a local sense of community and social capital: 'We say hello when we meet people in [this small town]'. At that time, I think that description was very accurate. However, in recent years, things appear to have changed. People are no longer greeting others along the paths of the small town as frequently as they used to some years ago. I have no clear explanation for this, but it is possible that the growth of the built-up environment that rapidly both increased the small town's population and changed the physical environment led to loss of social capital.

4. Concluding discussion

The continuous changes to the physical environments in the small town are clearly affecting how the socio-physical aspects together form environmental child friendliness (Kreutz, 2014; Kyttä, 2004; Jansson et al., 2022). Open spaces tend to be arenas for developing local social capital through various processes and practices (Morrow, 1999). The provision of a variety of spaces, the temporary changes there, and the promotion of independent mobility (Kyttä, 2004) through mainly limited car traffic can be a support, while there are also factors that appear to limit the local social capital. These factors include the very fast densification projects, the introduction of more car traffic there, and the destruction of sites that have been interesting to children and supportive for building and maintaining social capital. Changes in the physical environment thereby appear to have led to changes in local social capital and child friendliness over time.

The small town is an example of how planning ideals have changed in Sweden, leading to transformations of the former welfare era landscapes into something else (Qviström, 2022). In this particular case, despite having a local train station which is connected to ideas such as transit-oriented development (Jansson & Sunding, 2024), the transformation has not been into a very dense high-rise environment. Still, the small town is becoming both denser and more organised and formal, leaving less room for children both to roam and to meet with others in the local environment. Furthermore, it risks leaving less room for the temporary changes that appear to be of great value for both children in their play and for the building of social capital in general. Children's diminished access to informal and abandoned areas, which they had greatly appreciated (Jansson et al., 2016), appears to be affecting them in particular. This risks changing how they relate to the environment as actors (Wales et al., 2021) and agents of change (Malone, 2013),

Still, new arenas are being created such as mainly the new park, which could with time provide opportunities for developing a sense of community and children's social capital in various ways, with peers as well as others (Pacilli et al., 2013), as various functions can support each other (Sundevall & Jansson, 2020). A key question might be if the changes in the environments, including car traffic, might affect the levels of children's independent mobility in the small town, something which according to Porskamp et al. (2019) is a main driver of loss of social capital. This shows the importance of both social and physical environments in the creation of child-friendly environments, where children's play, mobility, and social lives are highly intertwined (Johansson et al., 2020). The small town, despite signs of loss of environments, mobility, and social capital, still resembles a Bullerby as described by Kyttä (2004). The children still had comparably high independent mobility and could find various places to use in 2019, although not on the level found in 2014 (Jansson & Sunding, 2024).

The case of this small town in Sweden shows the importance of including many aspects in the work for child friendliness and social capital, where access to a variety of places and changes over time can be particularly valuable to include. This case also shows the importance of taking an interest in children's own perspectives in order to improve all aspects of child friendliness. Specifically, it points at the importance of the physical environment in building and rebuilding social capital for and by children and others. It forms an example of how many types of relations, between people as well as to the physical landscape, affect children's places and independent mobility over time, where environments supporting various uses affect the building of local social capital and child friendliness.

Grant information

This work was supported by JSPS KAKENHI Grant Number JP20H02323.

References

Björklid, P., & Gummesson, M. (2013). Children's independent mobility in Sweden. The Swedish transport administration. (trafikverket.se)

Eriksson, M., & Dahlblom, K. (2020). Children's perspectives on health-promoting living environments: The significance of social capital. *Social Science & Medicine*, 258, 113059.

Holt, N. L., Lee, H., Millar, C. A., & Spence, J. C. (2015). 'Eyes on where children play': A retrospective study of active free play. *Children's Geographies*, 13(1), 73–88. https://doi.org/10.1080/14733285.2013.828449

Jacobs, J. (1961). *The death and life of great American cities*. Random House.

Jansson, M., Herbert, E., Zalar, A., & Johansson, M. (2022). Child-friendly environments – what, how and by whom? *Sustainability*, 14, 4852. https://doi.org/10.3390/su14084852

Jansson, M., & Persson, B. (2010). Playground planning and management: An evaluation of standard-influenced provision through user needs. *Urban Forestry & Urban Greening*, 9(1), 33–42.

Jansson, M., Sundevall, E., & Wales, M. (2016). The role of green spaces and their management in a child-friendly urban village. *Urban Forestry & Urban Greening*, 18, 228–236. https://doi.org/10.1016/j.ufug.2016.06.014

Jansson, M., & Sunding, A. (2024). Children's everyday recreational mobilities – growing up in a densifying Swedish small town. *Local Environment*, 29(6), 705–721.

Johansson, M., Raustorp, A., Mårtensson, F., Boldemann, C., Sternudd C., & Kylin, M. (2011). Attitudal antecedents of children's sustainable everyday mobility. *Transport and Health Issues: Studies on Mobility and Transport Research*, 3, 55–68.

Johansson, M., Mårtensson, F., Jansson, M., & Sternudd C., (2020). Urban Space for Children on the Move. In E. Owen D. Waygood, Margareta Friman, Lars E. Olsson, and Raktim Mitra (Eds.), *Transportation and Children's Well-Being*, 217–235. Amsterdam, Netherlands: Elsevier.

Kreutz, A. (2014). Lack of child-environment congruence in Cherbourg, Australia: Obstacles to well-being in an indigenous community. *Children, Youth and Environments*, 24, 53–81.

Kyttä, M. (2004). The extent of children's independent mobility and the number of actualized affordances as criteria for child-friendly environments. *Journal of Environmental Psychology*, 24, 179–198.

Littke, H. (2015). Planning the green walkable city: Conceptualizing values and conflicts for urban green space strategies in Stockholm. *Sustainability*, 7(8). https://doi.org/10.3390/su70811306

Malone, K. (2013). "The future lies in our hands": Children as researchers and environmental change agents in designing a child-friendly neighbourhood. *Local Environment*, 18(3), 372–395. https://doi.org/10.1080/13549839.2012.719020

Marzi, I., & Reimes, A. K. (2018). Children's independent mobility: Current knowledge, future directions, and public health implications. *International Journal of Environmental Research and Public Health*, *15*(11), 2441. https://doi.org/10.3390/ijerph15112441

Morrow, V. (1999). Conceptualising social capital in relation to the well-being of children and young people: A critical review. *The Sociological Review*, *47*(4), 744–765. https://doi.org/10.1111/1467–954X.00194

Mullenbach, L. E., Larson, L. R., Floyd, M. F., Marquet, O., Huang, J.-H., Alberico, C., Ogletree, S. S., & Hipp, J. A. (2022). Cultivating social capital in diverse, low-income neighborhoods: The value of parks for parents with young children. *Landscape and Urban Planning*, *219*, 104313. https://doi.org/10.1016/j.landurbplan.2021.104313

Nolin, C. (2016). Hundra år av lekplatshistoria 1850–1950. In M. Jansson & Å. K. Ahlklo (Eds.), *Plats för lek. Svenska lekplatser förr och nu* (pp. 34–55). Svensk Byggtjänst.

Pacilli, M. G., Giovannelli, I., Prezza, M., & Augimeri, M. L. (2013). Children and the public realm: Antecedents and consequences of independent mobility in a group of 11–13-year-old Italian children. *Children's Geographies*, *11*(4), 377–393. https://doi.org/10.1080/14733285.2013.812277

Porskamp, T., Ergler, C., Pilot, E., Sushama, P., & Mandic, S. (2019). The importance of social capital for young People's active transport and independent mobility in rural Otago, New Zealand. *Health & Place*, *60*, 102216.

Prezza, M., Alparone, F. R., Cristallo, C., & Luigi, S. (2005). Parental perception of social risk and of positive potentiality of outdoor autonomy for children: The development of two instruments. *Journal of Environmental Psychology*, *25*(4), 437–453. https://doi.org/10.1016/j.jenvp.2005.12.002

Pries, J., & Qviström, M. (2021). The patchwork planning of a welfare landscape: Reappraising the role of leisure planning in the Swedish welfare state. *Planning Perspectives*, *1*, 26.

Qviström, M. (2022). Finding the pulse of the welfare landscape: Reframing green space provision in modernist planning. *Geografiska Annaler: Series B, Human Geography*, *104*(3), 269–284. https://doi.org/10.1080/04353684.2022.2040376

Stone, M. R., Faulker, G. E., Mitra, R., & Buliung, R. N. (2014). The freedom to explore: Examining the influence of independent mobility on weekday, weekend and after-school physical activity behaviour in children living in urban and inner-suburban neighbourhoods of varying socioeconomic status. *International Journal of Behavioral Nutrition and Physical Activity*, *11*(5). https://link.springer.com/article/10.1186/1479-5868-11-5

Sundevall, E. P., & Jansson, M. (2020). Inclusive parks across ages: Multifunction and urban open space management for children, adolescents, and the elderly. *International Journal of Environmental Research and Public Health*, *17*(24), 9357. https://doi.org/10.3390/ijerph17249357

Veitch, J., Carver, A., Salmon, J., Abbott, G., Ball, K., Crawford, D., Cleland, V., & Timperio, A. (2017). What predicts children's active transport and independent mobility in disadvantaged neighborhoods? *Health & Place*, *44*, 103–109. https://doi.org/10.1016/j.healthplace.2017.02.003

Wales, M., Mårtensson, F., & Jansson, M. (2021). 'You can be outside a lot': Independent mobility and agency among children in a suburban community in Sweden. *Children's Geographies*, *19*(2), 184–196.

Wilhjelm, H. (2002). *Barn og omgivelser – virkelighet med flere fortolkninger* [Doctoral dissertation, Oslo School of Architecture].

Wood, L., Giles-Corti, B., Zubrick, S. R., & Bulsara, M. K. (2013). "Through the kids . . . we connected with our community": Children as catalysts of social capital. *Environment and Behavior*, *45*(3), 344–368. https://doi.org/10.1177/0013916511429329

8

BULLERBY CHILDREN IN TODAY'S JAPAN

How they play and who supports them

Mari Yoshinaga

1. Introduction

The perspective that societies can increase order, vibrancy, health, and comfort by creating connections between people has been noted by renowned researchers in various disciplines; Kinoshita noted this in Chapter 2 in a different context. Tocqueville (1805–1859) stated that volunteer organisations were the true source of America's strong civil society, while Dewey (1859–1952) noted that the vitality and depth of proximate and direct interaction and attachment were preconditions for social connectedness. In addition, Putnam (1926–2016) argued that health, well-being, education, economic productivity, and trust had declined due to the breakdown of communities and decline in civic engagement, which he attributed to a growing crisis. In fact, no significant decline in social activity occurred in American society, only a slight change in time spent with friends and neighbours and in membership in traditional volunteer organisations.

However, the number of people for whom the place of interaction was the Internet rather than restaurants/bars and, moreover, people for whom most people could not be trusted increased; as Klinenberg (1970–) puts it, the moral call for 'increased public involvement' did not lead to a significant increase in human connections, and informal social relational capital (social trust, the frequency of informal connections with the surroundings), which is essential for children's development, is difficult to rebuild. Rather, possibilities can be found of creating social connections and building communities and opportunities for civic participation (hereafter social infrastructure) by devising places where people will spend their time.

Jacobs (1916–2016) held this perspective, describing streets as important because (i) the presence of people on the streets maintains security; (ii) people come and go and meet each other, and trust grows; and (iii) children who grow up playing on the streets and watching adults in action learn the importance of engaging with people (children) who are not directly involved. Based on this problem consciousness, we conducted a multifaceted study to elucidate the spatial and temporal elements of the neighbourhood environment and other factors that contribute to the social relational capital of child development. One of the issues we addressed in this study is that with the declining birth rate, the presence of children is becoming less visible, and opportunities for children's opinions to be reflected in town planning are scarce; this leads to the loss of suitable environments for child-rearing. In this chapter, therefore, I discuss two points using data.

First, I use case studies to describe the realities of children in modern-day kayak villages as manifested in a generational playground map, a ground-breaking method for realising that children's presence is becoming harder to see. Although the population of children playing outside is declining, there are children who, if adults listen attentively, will talk about their own daily adventure stories and 'play stories', along with giving information about their geographical environments. Although these children do not have the same exciting experiences as the children in the noisy villages, they are making as much 'noise' as possible in the current playground environment while contending with negative factors such as urbanisation, an over-emphasis on academic achievement, and a declining birth rate.

Here, I aim to show these as play stories in connection with characteristic spaces. The method I used to obtain the data was the playground map survey. The children were asked to draw their own playground maps with information on playgrounds, play contents, and playmates, which they could then look at while being interviewed about the content and actual conditions of the play activities described. By comparing the two maps, it was possible to see the changes in playgrounds and play activities over a generation, 30 years. If one makes a map of playgrounds in the same area of their grandfather's generation and compares them, they will be aware of the changes in the playground environment over two generations (i.e. about 60 years).

The next task is to consider the need for adults who understand, sympathise with, and support children's *yakamashi* (here, I use *yakamashi* as a translation of Bullerby that is a Japanese noun meaning 'lively and energetic') in Bullerby Village. Are there necessary conditions to be an adult involved with children in the town? Despite the points made by our predecessors at the beginning regarding the importance of social relational capital, social connections, and social infrastructure, the demographic group of adults who are willing to take on this role themselves seems to continue growing. Some child-related professionals and civic activists feel a sense of crisis about this situation and are making efforts to publicise and share children's rights, create legal frameworks such as ordinances, and ensure that children have opportunities to play and experience nature and society in their immediate environments. Increasing the numbers of people interested in children and the environments of their upbringing and involving them in supportive activities is essential for building social capital that has a positive impact on child development.

The proportion of respondents who answered 'I think it is an easy country to have and raise children' was significantly lower than it is in other countries because respondents at the time did not perceive society as being supportive of child-rearing, as observed by the following other low ratings on the survey: 'Because the local community helps me raise my child' (5.5%) and 'Because society as a whole is kind and understanding towards having and raising children' (8.6%). These items related to the social capital of child-rearing have declined further, while the availability of childcare and other services have risen since the same survey in 2015 (Cabinet Office, 2020). It is not easy to change the attitudes of people who are not involved with children on a daily basis. Effective measures to increase people's interest in the child-rearing environment must be initiated as soon as possible, but the examination of the relevant factors has not been sufficient. Therefore, using data from a large-scale online survey (online survey) that was conducted as the first step in the project Social Relationship Capital for Child Development, I focus in this study on the characteristics of childhood experienced by people who work with children, analysing and discussing the following factors that may have led to an interest in child-rearing.

Let us consider the first issue: the stories of children found on playground maps depicting modern-day yakamashi, Bullerby Village.

2. Stories from modern Japan's yakamashi, Bullerby Village

Playing in the base

Children long to have places of their own, special places where no one can disturb them, where they can hide their secrets without the risk of being discovered by their parents or other adults or where they can speak a few bad words or do something rash without being offended or complaining. Sometimes one gets the opportunity to have such a place. If they happen to go out and find a little hidden space where they can shelter from the rain – a place to put their things that are not easily seen – it becomes a base for the child alone. Children wander around, keep an eye on the surroundings, play or go home from school and collect trees, leaves, grass and even little sticks and cloth they pick up from around the area to make parts of the base. Even if the place is almost finished, a little building process is essential to make it their own.

A map of children's playgrounds in the Heisei era, which was started in 2006, shows a place in the corner of a vast private school yard that can be entered through a hole in the wire mesh fence as a base for children. In the interviews about this place, the children also revealed their feelings of not wanting adults to identify the place. They said they brought cardboard, blankets, and flashlights into the space, which was a few square metres, and sometimes they even ate snacks there.

We accompanied the children to their playgrounds and collected data to create a playground map. In a similar way, Karsten (2005), who conducted a survey of children's use of space, noted that children's territories are freer and wider when they play a lot outside. Over the years, children's territories have become narrower (Gaster, 1991; Hillman et al., 1990; Pooley et al., 2005), which was also revealed in the Dutch street survey by Lia Karsten (2005) and others. These results provide a basis for placing the retention of child-friendly outdoor play spaces at the top of the policy agenda.

Walk as a cat

In planning roads to and around school routes and playgrounds (parks, open spaces where children gather, adventure playgrounds), it is important to take into account children's characteristics, such as their desire to follow narrow paths and their willingness to try climbing to high places. For example, children move like cats in areas such as loopholes and through-hole paths.

Two reasons seem to underlie these behaviours. One is a playful, child-like love of exploration and adventure; children are motivated by an uncontrollable curiosity and a desire to challenge themselves. The other possible explanation is that children have an intrinsic desire for very small spaces. Children's facilities in Düsseldorf and Cologne, Germany, which I visited during my research, had 'calming rooms' where children could sit, lie down, or get into a slightly smaller space. The Japanese national facility for children with medical care called Momiji (Maple) House, at the National Centre for Child Health and Development, also had a slightly smaller space, but with flashing lights and other peculiar innovations. Spatial innovations can be helpful for psychological calm and concentration to inhibit behaviour and for relaxation. Such a background may also be present in the characteristics of children's desire to go through loopholes, high places, and narrow spaces in outdoor play. This may be a type of behaviour or movement that is consistent with the idea of sensory integration.

Observing children playing with these spaces and tools, one can see how they successfully help younger children with less physical strength, mobility, and judgement and how they enjoy the company of their slightly slower-moving friends. Complex, child-favourite, space, and town tools also naturally foster children's peer relationships.

Creating parks with children's participation

A survey of children's playgrounds in various towns reveals that they are the most common places for children to play outside of their own homes and friends' homes, followed by paths, schoolyards, and relatives' homes, all of which are characteristic of each town. However, parks in developed countries – especially in Japan – have many signs with detailed instructions and prohibitions, such as 'No ball playing', 'No noise', 'Do not play in the fountain', 'Do not enter the grass', and 'Push the bicycle by hand' seemingly aimed at children. In fact, if a child violates even the slightest sign (for example, playing with a ball in a park where ball playing is prohibited), someone watching from somewhere will call the city hall or a nearby school and complain that the child is breaking the rule. Then, city hall officials are forced to make another large, conspicuous sign and erect it, filling the park with signs stating what is prohibited.

Some parks have implemented the idea of making the space, rules for use, and placement of signs and playground equipment reflect the opinions of children about what they use. Although the Convention on the Rights of the Child states that children's opinions on what they use and where must be reflected, in practice, this is extremely rare because it is seldom realised. I conducted and analysed a follow-up survey and found that children involved in this experience had an increased sense of self-efficacy, a heightened sense of community empowerment, and a more promising presence as future leaders of community development (Yoshinaga et al., 2014).

3. Becoming adults involved with children in the town: what kind of adults are those in Bullerby Village?

The childhood of the adults in Bullerby Village

The adults I refer to here as 'the adults of Bullerby Village' do not refer to the adults themselves who live in Lindgren's Bullerby Village (Lindgren, 1988b): they are the fathers, mothers, and a grandfather of three families of six children, each of whom looks after the children's development and respects their independence and autonomy. They respect their roles as helpers and tolerate a little mischief and misbehaviour. If children seem to be having trouble, these adults do not do everything for them but give them advice on how to manage it better or give them a little help and push them to do the rest on their own.

Adults like this exist in modern Japan; for example, free playgrounds known as adventure playgrounds and playparks have playworkers, specialists in their field who gently support children so that they can enjoy outdoor play. In children's centres and cafés, professionals ensure and oversee the activities that are essential for children's survival, such as play and food.

These 'people who work with children' can be regarded as the adults of the 'noisy village' in contemporary Japan. What kinds of childhoods did they have and how did they get to where they are today? In a joint research project with Kinoshita et al., I first conducted an online survey as a preliminary study, which was disseminated via the research members' social networking services. The majority of the subjects were people who work with children, and I statistically examined their characteristics.

I conducted a pilot survey online in March 2021 to scrutinise the selection of questions prior to the online survey and the paper survey, which controlled for age and other attribute biases. Links were disseminated on the project website and members' social networking sites to collect as many responses as possible. The main items are summarised in Table 8.1.

TABLE 8.1 Items on the Online Survey.

Attributes	*Gender, Age, Work*
The social infrastructure in the nurturing environment (playgrounds and bases)	1. entrance to or around home 2. road in front of or near home or estate site 3. friends' homes and surroundings 4. park 5. school grounds 6. fields 7. river or pond 8. field or open space 9. children's centre 10. candy shop 11. shop (supermarket or games centre) 12. community meeting place 13. shrine or temple grounds 14. parking lot, secret availability of bases
Play content	1. playing tag or hide-and-seek 2. playing with a ball 3. playing with fruit 4. *menko* or spinning top 5. kicking stones or drawing on the ground 6. creating something with various objects around 7. climbing trees or high walls 8. running races 9. playing with bicycles or speed 10. playing make-believe and dolls 11. video games
Social capital: how to engage with the community	1. let friends into your own house/yard (grounds) 2. go into your neighbour's friend's house/yard (grounds) 3. greet your neighbour's friend's parents 4. greet your neighbour (not your friend's parents) 5. go inside your neighbour's house/yard 6. listen to your neighbour (not your friend's parents) or tell your own story 7. help you with your problems and advice 8. help neighbours (e.g. watering flowers, holding things) 9. play with neighbour's children 10. participate in own festivals/events such as neighbourhood association (housing complex, company housing) 11. participate in communal work such as cleaning activities such as neighbourhood association (housing complex, company housing) 12. annoy adults 13. play pranks or do something a bit wrong

(Continued)

TABLE 8.1 (Continued)

Attributes	Gender, Age, Work
What kind of people were in the neighbourhood?	1. people who (seem to) call out to us when they see us 2. people who look after us on the way to and from school 3. people who teach us various games 4. people who do interesting and fun things for us 5. people who make things, fix things, and teach us various skills 6. people who praise us for our good qualities 7. people who (seem to) help me with my problems or concerns 8. people who share something they have made or something interesting with me for my children 9. people who allow my children free access to their house or garden 10. people who get angry with me or warn me when I misbehave or do something naughty 11. people who gather my children and take them to nature experiences such as camping 12. people who take the children on camping or other nature experiences
Was your childhood significantly influenced by neighbourhood adults or the environment?	1. Yes ☐ 2. No ☐

Play environment, play content, and relationships with neighbours as social capital

I received 2,257 responses to this survey, and I divided the respondents into two groups: those who were involved in work or activities related to children (child-related workers) and others. A chi-square test of the proportion of yes responses showed significant differences, but the effect sizes were mostly small. Responses with small effect sizes are shown in Table 8.2.

Table 8.2 shows that child-related workers were more likely to have engaged in or experienced certain engagements and relationships. I performed logistic regression analysis to determine which if any factors contributed most to these adults having become activists for children. Specifically, I selected explanatory variables that I had determined to be highly relevant and then set up a model to analyse them; Table 8.3 shows the results. I found that 'Climbing trees/tall walls' and 'Someone who praises you for your good qualities' increased the likelihood of becoming an activist for children, while 'Watching you go to and from school' had the opposite effect. A test of the fitness of the model (Hosmer and Lemeshow's examination) indicated significant fit ($\chi^2 = 26.53$; $p < .001$).

TABLE 8.2 Childhood Play among Child-related Workers and Other Adults.

	Child-related workers	Others	χ^2	p	Effect size	Cramer V
Content of play						
Finding and eating berries	65.1%	53.7%	30.438	***	small	0.12
Kicking stones and drawing on the ground	65.1%	52.0%	40.47	***	small	0.14
Tree climbing and high wall climbing	53.5%	43.5%	22.53	***	small	0.10
Playing make-believe and dolls	45.3%	35.3%	23.4	***	small	0.11
Relations with neighbours						
Entering the property	57.1%	44.7%	34.76	***	small	0.13
Listening to a story	54.3%	40.9%	40.38	***	small	0.14
Sharing souvenirs	43.6%	31.4%	35.76	***	small	0.13
Helping household	29.2%	19.6%	27.94	***	small	0.11
Playing with kids	60.9%	49.4%	30.2	***	small	0.12
Encouraged by neighbours						
Praising your good points	33.6%	22.8%	32.143	***	small	0.12
Letting you come and go freely	31.2%	21.7%	26.053	***	small	0.11

4. Being like Pippi

In another of Lindgren's famous tales, Pippi is a tremendously powerful, red-haired, independently living character who wears unpaired socks (Lindgren, 1988a). She is portrayed as a sweetheart who gets on well with the two thin kids who live next door, Tommy and Annika, and she invites them to try adventures and challenges they have never experienced before. At the same time, Pippi encourages Tommy and Annika to try and fail. Of course, Tommy and Annika do not have Pippi's range of life experiences; thus, they are timid and hesitant about everything and fail at first. However, Pippi does not care about that at all and is not overly concerned, encouraging them to move on and try again. Is there anyone like Pippi around children in our society today?

Here I introduce a professional staff member who was born in Setagaya Ward, on the western edge of Tokyo. His nickname is Kanpei, and his

TABLE 8.3 Childhood Play Factors Associated with Becoming a Child-related Worker.

	β	Wald	Degree of freedom	p	OR	95% CI Range	
Gender	−0.62	31.09	1.00	**	0.54	0.43	0.67
Age under 30 or over 40	0.38	13.10	1.00	**	1.46	1.19	1.79
Tag or hide-and-seek	−0.05	0.20	1.00	ns	0.95	0.76	1.19
Ball playing	−0.17	2.70	1.00	ns	0.84	0.69	1.03
Finding and eating berries	0.14	1.83	1.00	ns	1.15	0.94	1.40
Menko or spinning top	−0.03	0.07	1.00	ns	0.97	0.80	1.18
Kicking stones and drawing on the ground	0.24	5.12	1.00	*	1.28	1.03	1.57
Creating something with various objects around	−0.11	1.10	1.00	ns	0.89	0.72	1.10
Tree climbing and high wall climbing	0.35	11.46	1.00	**	1.42	1.16	1.73
Running races	0.09	0.55	1.00	ns	1.09	0.87	1.38
Playing with bicycles or speed	0.04	0.21	1.00	ns	1.04	0.87	1.26
Playing make-believe and doll	0.03	0.07	1.00	ns	1.03	0.84	1.26
Playing at the secret base	0.23	5.67	1.00	*	1.26	1.04	1.53

* $p<.05$, ** $p<0.001$

professional title is outdoor play promoter (Figure 8.1), similar to a community playworker. These workers are not merely there to let the children who come to the playpark experience outdoor play; they involve the adults around the children, making people from all over the city get to know each other so that the community can be positive about children playing outside and bringing together the people who run the place with those who want to use it. In addition, they do other valuable community work.

I see these professionals as the Pippi Longstockings of modern society. Children are surrounded by overprotective adults who instil a fear of failure in them before they even begin to try, and these workers act as attractive role models who make them want to try and encourage them to have new experiences. If every town in the world had an outdoor play promoter, children would be able to play more independently and freely than they do now.

FIGURE 8.1 Community play worker: Kanpei the outdoor play promoter.

My research data on child-related workers also show that to become such professionals, it is important for these adults to grow up in communities where they are allowed to experience 'tree climbing and high wall climbing' at an early age, without 'praising good things' or pointing out dangers first. From now on, we should behave as such persons who support children, with one eye on the danger and the other on the ground, as Pippi. I assure you that we must do so if we are to ensure the survival of the children of Bullerby Village in our world.

Conclusion

In this chapter, I described the importance of documenting stories of children's play in contemporary society, where children are becoming less visible. I described a case study of conducting a playground survey based on careful interviews and observations and incorporated the information into a map to provide evidence that children's play is inspired by the spatial characteristics and things in the town. Next, focusing on the adults who support the lives of children in Bullerby Village, I presented the results of a survey conducted on the childhood experiences of people who had chosen as adults to work supporting children's play. They had childhood experiences of spontaneous play such as tree climbing and writing graffiti on the road that carried a danger of being scolded by adults. Rich childhood experiences appear to be one of the motivators of pursuing child-supportive work when they grow up. Finally, in reference to Pippi the Longshanks, the significance of a device in which personnel such as community playworkers push the backs of children and send them out to play was described.

Grant information

This work was supported by JSPS KAKENHI Grant Number JP20H02323.

Acknowledgements

In writing this chapter, I have drawn much inspiration from Ms Lindgren's story. For many years, the kids in Bullerby Village and Pippi have helped children to imagine exciting worlds and to feel as if they were really there. Even as adults, we will never forget that imaginative experience. The study would not have been possible without the cooperation of the many 'children in the past' who took part in the online survey. I would also like to thank Kanpei for gently encouraging children like Pippi on the playground and for his new work in creating happiness and connection among adults, and I look forward to supporting him in his future endeavours.

References

Cabinet Office. (2020). *Report of the 2020 international attitude survey on society with a declining birthrate*. Retrieved February 29, 2024, from https://warp.da.ndl.go.jp/info:ndljp/pid/13024511/www8.cao.go.jp/shoushi/shoushika/research/r02/kokusai/pdf/zentai/s2_6.pdf

Gaster, S. (1991). Urban children's access to the neighbourhood: Changes over three generations. *Environment and Behavior, 23*(1), 70–85.

Hillman, M., Adams J., & Whitelegg, J. (1990). *One false move: A study on children's independent mobility*. Policy Studies Institute.

Karsten, L. (2005). It all used to be better? Different generations on continuity and change in urban children's daily use of space. *Children's Geographies, 3*(3), 275–290.

Lindgren, L. (1988a). *Pippi longstocking* (Reissue). Puffin Books.

Lindgren, L. (1988b). *The children of noisy village* (Illustrated version). Puffin Books.

Pooley, C., Turnbull, J., & Adams, A. (2005). The journey to school in Britain since the 1940s: Continuity and change. *Area, 37*(1), 43–53.

Yoshinaga, M., Takeda, Y., & Kinoshita, I. (2014). Effects of participation in community activities on self-efficacy of Japanese junior high school students. *Global Journal of Community Psychology Practice, 5*(2), 1–12.

PART IV
Streets, parks, and neighbourhoods

9
CHILDREN'S OUTDOOR PLAY AND SOCIAL CAPITAL

Insights from one London housing scheme

Tim Gill

1. **Children's outdoor play, and social capital: revisiting Jane Jacobs**

Jacobs on urban children's spatial lives

One striking yet rarely discussed feature of Jane Jacobs' seminal book on urban life and city design, *The Death and Life of Great American Cities*, is her interest in children. She devotes a whole chapter (indeed the fourth chapter out of 22) to the topic of how urban children grow up to be healthy, engaged, responsible citizens of big cities. The main thesis of that chapter is evident from its title: 'The uses of sidewalks: assimilating children'. In it, Jacobs argues that children come to learn what she calls 'the first fundamental' of urban life: that 'people must take a modicum of public responsibility for each other even if they have no ties to each other', largely through their informal, often playful interactions with adults in shared public spaces (pre-eminently, sidewalks) beyond their immediate family and school/childcare settings. Jacobs explicitly rejects the idea that this principle can be learnt within more conventional sites of learning such as home and school and also the idea that it can be learnt in conventional playgrounds (Jacobs, 1961, p. 82). She also extends the argument to include teenagers, saying that they are 'always being criticized for . . . loitering, but they can hardly grow up without it. The trouble comes when it is done not within society, but as a form of outlaw life' (Jacobs, 1961, p. 86).

Jacobs argues here that shared encounters between children and adults – including conflicts and disagreements – are essential ingredients in helping children to understand their obligations and responsibilities to others beyond their home and the institutions in which they spend time, and also in helping them to understand the care, concern, and expectations that others hold for them. Hence for Jacobs, healthy social relations between children and adults are not a matter of eliminating encounters that some adults find annoying or upsetting. She sees such episodes as part of what helps children understand themselves as social beings, not as evidence of unacceptable behaviour or poor parenting. The public realm thus becomes an arena in which children rub along with others, in part through their play, and get to know what it means to get along with adults as well as with other children.

In her chapter, Jacobs is offering not an explicit theory but a narrative: a rich, intuitive story that aims to show how children, through their everyday encounters in public space, are both actors and learners in a web of social interactions, including obligations, responsibilities, and expectations. For Jane Jacobs, these interactions both exemplify a lively, diverse, liveable urban neighbourhood and explain how people gradually learn to coexist in them. Her interest in the ways in which children learn, grow, and come to understand and engage with the people and places around them through their everyday experiences, including their outdoor play, foreshadows some of the key moves that emerged in childhood studies, children's geographies, and the sociology of childhood in the 1980s and more recently (Holloway & Valentine, 2000; James et al., 1990). Also underpinning the story are lines of thought from pedagogy, urban planning, and design, and implicit assumptions about society's obligations to children (including the obligation to provide space for play, which for Jacobs is as much a basic right as it is a developmentally beneficial process).

Children and social capital

The term social capital is 'an elusive concept' (Karsten, 2011). It is understood here as a label for the ways that individuals improve their lives through active engagement with their social networks. Using a metaphorical allusion to financial capital, it points to how trust, mutual support, and reciprocal relationships and obligations outside of close family networks act as resources for societies and communities as well as for the individuals who are part of them.

Robert Putnam, the pre-eminent theorist of social capital, pays tribute to Jacobs, calling her 'one of the inventors' of the term (Putnam, 2000, p. 308). Yet Putnam's own scholarly works, and those of other leading social capital theorists, offer a simpler story around children's places in social relations than does Jacobs. They largely frame children as mere passive recipients of adult social exchange systems. Where children's agency is under discussion, it is typically problematised; for example, Coleman (1988) – in a clear contrast with Jacobs' position – sees peer group interaction largely as a form of anti-social behaviour that leads to the development of alternative values and norms (Weller & Bruegel, 2009). There is little consideration of the learning and developmental pathways children might take by being a part of social exchanges in their communities, as both givers and recipients of support from neighbours and strangers, and of how these might shape their perspectives and understandings as they grow up.

As Weller and Bruegel (2009) note, scholars of social capital show little intrinsic interest in children. By contrast, in their own work, Weller and Bruegel argue that children directly forge relationships with children and adults that influence both their social relations and those of their parents. Similarly, Morrow and Karsten show in their research how children create and maintain their own social networks (although adults influence these processes) (Morrow, 1999; Karsten, 2011). However, while these scholars argue for seeing children as social agents, they do not examine in any detail the experiences and pathways by which children might become full participants in supportive social exchanges.

Doorstep space as a key spatial feature

This chapter takes as its starting point Jacobs' arguments about children's evolving sense of themselves as social beings who have connections that reach beyond home and school/childcare, building on the social capital critiques of Morrow, Karsten, and Weller and Bruegel. It brings into focus some threads of Jacobs' story – outdoor play, experiential learning, social relationships, and urban planning and design. And it explores how these threads relate to one housing scheme in London where the public realm includes a form of shared space that knits these threads together. That form is 'doorstep play space', meaning public or semi-public outdoor space that is intended for use by children at play but that is immediately adjacent to children's homes and hence easily accessible (and usually observable) from family dwellings. The term is used in regional planning guidance (Mayor of London, 2012).

Following Jacobs (1961), doorstep play space refers to the spatial qualities of neighbourhoods and how they influence interactions between children and adults, who are of primary interest here. In terms of space, the focus is on neighbourhood features that influence children's outdoor play. Hence in this chapter I draw on theoretical thinking on, and empirical studies of, outdoor play in public space.

In keeping with the United Nations Committee on the Rights of the Child, I hold that opportunities for children to play are created through the suitability of three broad components: space (i.e. a physical or virtual space within which children can play), time (i.e. a lack of competing demands for children's time), and adult attitudes (i.e. adult dispositions that are supportive or permissive of children playing, or at least not actively hostile to it).

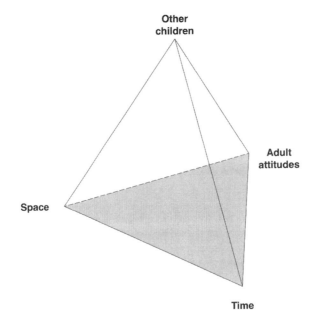

FIGURE 9.1 The play pyramid (see Gill, 2021, p. 27).

Illustrator credit: Sam Williams.

I also hold that for children, one critical if not essential feature of their playing lives is the presence of other children (UNCRC, 2013; Gill, 2021). This set of preconditions for play can be represented in pyramidical form (see Figure 9.1).

Empirical evidence

Empirical evidence shows links between several neighbourhood-built environment features and the time that children spend in outdoor play. Systematic literature reviews of this evidence base show that the most influential features concern neighbourhood traffic levels, emphasising the value of reducing road danger through such measures as ensuring traffic-free access to space for play (Lambert et al., 2019; Visser & van Aalst, 2022; Gemmell et al., 2023). Intriguingly, these same reviews find that when it comes to dedicated playgrounds, the evidence base for an influence is less clear-cut; some primary studies show an effect, while others do not.

There is also some empirical support for the role of outdoor play in shared public space in building social capital. One UK systematic literature review found that regular, two- to three-hour road closures in residential streets (a model for opening streets for play promoted by the NGO Playing Out) created 'new and important social connections between neighbours of all ages and strengthened existing relationships' (Bagnall et al., 2023, p. 43).

2. Methodology and structure of chapter

The rest of this chapter explores the links between children's play, shared outdoor space and social relations, drawing on a limited study of one housing scheme in London. I start with a thumbnail sketch describing the scheme's history, context, and physical features, focusing on its innovative public and semi-public outdoor spaces. I offer glimpses and insights into children's play and adult attitudes, drawing opportunistically on existing material provided by the local authority. A lack of research resources meant that I could not carry out any separate observations, surveys, or focus group activities. I also offer some necessarily exploratory discussion on the background and underlying mechanisms that might link children's play in the public realm with neighbourliness and social capital. The chapter concludes with wider thoughts on understanding social capital and the links with children's outdoor play in their neighbourhoods.

This chapter revisits ideas from my book *No Fear: Growing Up in a Risk Averse Society* about the emergence of an 'everyday morality' in children. I characterise this as

> the norms and conventions that shape much of social activity. This system of rules ... comes into play when deciding, among other things: whether or not to help someone we do not know; how to respond to a joke at our expense; when to stand up for ourselves and argue with someone we disagree with, and when it is better to back off; how to deal with the abuse of power; how far loyalty can justify actions that might harm those outside our circle; how to respond to, and where appropriate resist, peer pressure; whom we can trust and how far we can trust them.
>
> (Gill, 2007, p. 43)

While everyday morality is not equivalent to what Jacobs called the first fundamental of city life, it does encompass similar notions of connection, reciprocity, and mutual obligations. Moreover, both concepts recognise that social norms do not exist solely as abstract principles but are manifest in our daily actions and choices.

3. The Kings Crescent housing scheme: a thumbnail sketch

History, context

King's Crescent is a regeneration housing project in North London. The site was originally a post-war public housing estate built by the London Borough of Hackney consisting of around 620 homes in 11 apartment blocks, including two tower blocks. By the 1990s, the poor construction of the tower blocks had become evident, and the wider estate had fallen into disrepair. The estate's evolution since then has been unusually protracted, due to several failed attempts at regeneration, the global financial crisis of 2008–2010, and more recently the COVID-19 pandemic. Indeed, at the time of writing, construction on site has not finished (with the next phase of works set to begin on or after Spring 2025). In 2012 (some years after the two tower blocks were demolished), a public–private partnership was set up similar to many other estate regeneration schemes in London. Some of the remaining blocks were subsequently demolished, others refurbished, and new blocks constructed, resulting in a mix of social housing, shared ownership units, and private for sale units, including significant numbers suitable for families. In addition, the public spaces and courtyards have been reconfigured and redesigned (London Borough of Hackney, n.d.).

King's Crescent involved an extensive design process including both design review with experts (of whom I was one, giving my time pro bono) and community engagement with both adults and children. The public realm design was taken forward by an experienced and committed practice that has designed innovative play spaces in other schemes in London (Muf Architecture/Art, n.d.). The level of attention to children's play throughout the master planning and public realm design process was unusually high. The design approach, which I describe shortly, was also radical. Rather than follow the conventional formula of dedicated or formal play areas, it aimed to create multi-functional spaces that allow and encourage children to play while also catering for other social and outdoor activities. In particular, the inclusion of a permanent play street with explicit play features, labelled as such, was and is a provocative move that poses wider cultural and policy questions about the relative priority given to cars versus children; it was described by one member of the design team as 'polemical' and 'a postcard from the future' (personal communication 27/10/2021).

As well as the play street – created in an existing street that was once part of the road network and is now closed to through traffic as part of the redesign – the outdoor space includes three enclosed, semi-private courtyards. The street and courtyards are all easily accessible from family dwellings and free from traffic dangers. Each courtyard includes various forms of seating, a lighting scheme, and some space adjacent to some of the ground-floor residential units that is for the sole use of those residents (with their boundaries defined by low walls). The overall result is to create a set of doorstep play spaces adjacent to private garden space which, compared with conventional play areas, have the potential to increase the likelihood of interactions between children and adults, in particular interactions involving non-caregivers (see Figure 9.2 for an aerial overview, Figure 9.3 for a plan, and Figures 9.4–9.10 for more aerials and site photos).

Children's outdoor play and social capital 135

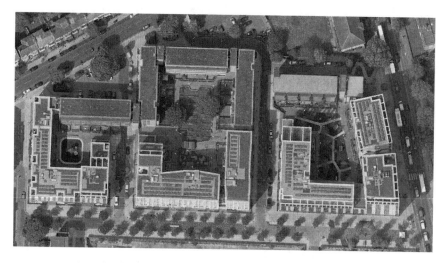

FIGURE 9.2 Aerial overview of part of the Kings Crescent development as c. 2021.
Source: Google Maps.

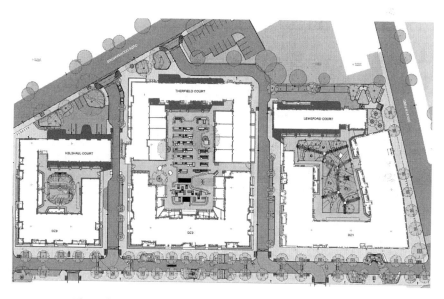

FIGURE 9.3 Plan of part of the Kings Crescent development, showing the 3 courtyards and (at bottom) play street.
Source: muf architecture/art.

136 Tim Gill

FIGURES 9.4–9.5 Photos of Murrain Road play street, Kings Crescent.
Credits: Lewis Ronald (top photo), Tim Gill (bottom photo).

Play street (Murrain Road)

In the play street, traditional play equipment including a hammock swing is combined with less prescriptive elements (a raised table, a small brick stage/theatre structure, natural play opportunities from planted beds, willow structures, logs, rocks, and a water supply), and seating. The tarmac surface is decorated with random white lines, in a playful nod to conventional street markings. Some time after the play street was reopened, a barrier was installed to stop vehicle traffic from coming in from a busier road. The play street design generated management and maintenance issues, with one item of equipment (a circular metal structure labelled the tiara by the design team, and installed in the street) being removed because of safety concerns.

Courtyard 1

Courtyard 1 is the smallest courtyard, with a raised, surfaced play space including a wide slide, small stepping logs, and an extended bench.

FIGURE 9.6 Photo of Courtyard 1, Kings Crescent.
Credit: Lewis Ronald.

Courtyard 2

Courtyard 2 is the largest courtyard. Some of the central space is given over to a grassy area with raised growing beds and garden sheds, surrounded by a low brick wall. Another walled grassy area includes raised metal platforms with gaps between them. The rest of the space includes a swing and several climbable boulders. Encircling these two grassy spaces, and more or less defining the perimeter of the courtyard, is a flat, hard-surfaced path that is suitable for scooters and bikes. This path includes a metal structure designed to look like a start/finish line.

FIGURES 9.7–9.8   Photos of Courtyard 2, Kings Crescent.

Credit: Lewis Ronald.

Courtyard 3

Courtyard 3 is roughly L-shaped, with a mix of grassy and softfall surfacing, partitioned by a set of connected, solid raised pathways. Several play structures are dotted around the courtyard, including spinning disks, a raised wooden platform, and a large fallen tree trunk.

FIGURES 9.9–9.10 Photos of Courtyard 3, Kings Crescent.
Credit: Lewis Ronald.

4. Children's play on the scheme and adult attitudes

Reaction to the scheme

The Kings Crescent scheme scores well in local authority feedback for its children's play provision. It has won architectural and housing design awards and is included in best practice, policy, and guidance publications on child-friendly urban planning and design from the Greater London Authority, London Borough of Hackney, and other sources (Publica & Erect Architecture, 2019; Gill, 2021; London Borough of Hackney, 2021).

However there has been a mixed reaction to the designs from adult residents. This is especially true of the play street but also of some of the courtyards. The London Borough of Hackney carried out a post-occupation evaluation of the scheme in around 2021. Below, I give a sample of adult resident feedback quotes from this evaluation, thematically grouped according to the underlying attitude. In summarising this feedback, one municipal officer said that outdoor play was a topic that gave rise to sharply differing views from residents (personal communication 11/26/2021):

> Play scored above average [but] it also received many negative comments regarding the functionality of the equipment, anti-social behaviour, safety and materials. There is a split between residents who want more functional play and those who want to reduce noise.

Positive attitudes about play

> 'The children enjoy it [the play spaces]. Bit dubious about the "goal" in the other courtyard though'.
> 'Can't say I understand all the items on play street but kids seem to like them'.
> 'Feel very lucky to live here, the play street [is] brilliant!'

Negative attitudes about play

> 'The noise coming from the courtyard is just unbelievable. Having a close courtyard with play equipment in the middle is not a good idea'.
> 'The play street, on which Hackney put so much positive focus, is a nuisance for the people who actually live here'.
> 'The play street has now been taken over by skateboarders'.
> 'The play street, whilst having benefit to local children, has been a real problem for residents. It encourages anti-social behaviour, loitering and littering. There is always so much rubbish being left around and large groups either around the benches and other play facilities often late into

the night. The estate has turned into a skatepark, again resulting in lots of noise and degrading the pavements'.

Mixed or unclear attitudes about play

'The play equipment is stylish but mostly not actually that fun . . . a swing set/slide etc would be good on play street'.

'The play equipment looks modern and quirky, but it bores children. The only one that children like is the hammock, but it is very uncomfortable. More traditional equipment, such as slides, climbing frames and see-saws would be much more fun for children'.

'The play things like the hammock aren't very user friendly. Seems like they are more for aesthetics'.

'Courtyard is like an architect's drawing, looks nice but serves no purpose. Subsequently unused'.

'Another issue is the play equipment which I think is very badly designed/planned. There is a football goal which means all the kids play football in the smallest space which is also right by some of the allotments so the plants we are growing are often damaged by footballs being kicked. I have also been told that there shouldn't be ball games played down there so have no idea why a football goal is part of the play equipment. There is then just one swing, which is fine but often there are lots of kids all piled onto it'.

Emerging themes from adult feedback

This limited survey of Kings Crescent shows that outdoor play is indeed supported by the design and management of the shared outdoor spaces. Furthermore, the resident feedback quoted shows a degree of tolerance of children's outdoor play in these spaces, alongside an expectation that children should have places to play near where they live. There is also some appreciation of the play facilities from adult residents (although also some differences of views on the design and play value of the play features themselves, a debate I will not pursue here).

The design and locations of these spaces clearly result in interactions between children at play and adult residents. They also generate some tensions and potential conflicts of varying degrees of seriousness (with the main concerns being noise and perceived antisocial behaviour). It is also clear from feedback that the multifunctional nature of the outdoor spaces has left some adult residents confused and dissatisfied. This was confirmed in an on-site discussion with both a municipal officer and a member of the design team that revealed anxiety about what they described as 'an ambiguous approach' to play on the scheme (personal communication 10/27/2021). However, in general, these conflicts and tensions appear to be resolvable by residents themselves.

It is important not to place inappropriate weight on these resident responses. Crucially, they do not include any views or comments from children. Moreover, they need to be seen in the light of the processes that generated them (in essence, an invitation from the local authority, which might be expected to lead to more negative than positive feedback). Respondents' attitudes may vary over time, and their opinions may be more nuanced than indicated by these short quotes.

Another important contextual factor in interpreting these responses is that (as already noted) the housing scheme was only partially built at the time of writing. In particular, several public spaces are planned that are likely to create more opportunities for play and socialising, which may have implications for the patterns of use in existing spaces (especially the play street, as it is currently the only shared, publicly accessible outdoor space on the estate).

5. Discussion

Insights from Kings Crescent

The approach to play space in the Kings Crescent scheme captures some of the features of sidewalks that Jacobs saw as socially significant, including convenience for play and the potential for frequent, varied, casual interactions between local children and adults who they do not have close ties with. Hence it is an opportunity to gain insights into how the experiences of children and adults in shared outdoor space might relate to the web of social activities that are implied in the idea of social capital.

Kings Crescent shows that public spaces in residential developments can be designed so that

- children will play in them regularly and their parents/carers will permit this even though they are not formal play areas;
- children's play will impinge on the daily lives of adult residents, giving rise to a degree of dissatisfaction and potential disagreement/conflict, as well as appreciation; and
- adult dissatisfaction will be accompanied by some acceptance and tolerance of children's presence.

Following on the last bullet point, Kings Crescent also contradicts the view that in designing public space for children's play, one goal should be eliminating any possible conflict or disagreement among residents. Indeed, as Jacobs suggested, and as I argued in *No Fear* (Gill, 2007, pp. 43–44), such disagreements can even be seen as features, not bugs, of public spaces: as a beneficial outcome of the shared outdoor space design, not an undesirable one (although some of the adult residents may not see it that way).

Doorstep play, everyday morality, and social capital: an emerging picture

The vignette offered by Kings Crescent begins to sketch out a picture about how, through play in shared public space, children come to acquire a sense of themselves as socially connected, active, and engaged moral agents. It suggests that play in doorstep play spaces gives rise to the kind of social interactions that might plausibly be key experiential ingredients in that process. This position on the relationship between experience and understanding is a central tenet of the sociology of childhood; children are not simple passive recipients of adult instruction, but are active in shaping, and making sense of, their own lives (James et al., 1990).

Earlier in this chapter, I argued that existing scholarly definitions and understandings of social capital pay little or no attention to children's social lives and their emerging senses of themselves as social agents with duties, responsibilities, and obligations to others. My conception of 'everyday morality' – influenced by Jacobs' work – can be seen as an attempt to fill this gap. However, the concept undeniably needs more fleshing out.

In particular, the differing social experiences of groups who are either privileged or marginalised through their ethnicity, class, or other group characteristics need close interrogation. Alongside this, scholars could gather and explore case studies and qualitative research drawn from social and educational psychology, sociologies of childhood and children's geographies, and urban design, among other disciplines, and quantitative longitudinal studies drawing on both existing publicly available data such as crime statistics and new data such as measures of levels of trust.

How and where do children learn about social connections and obligations and put this knowledge into practice? This chapter sketches out one possible answer: through frequent outdoor play in spaces that are close to home and shared with other adults. It is a short step from this question to wider concerns about civic and democratic values and ideas. These concerns, clearly evident in Jacobs' writings, are even more pressing in an interconnected world that faces existential global challenges around climate and the environment.

Grant information

This work was supported by JSPS KAKENHI Grant Number JP20H02323.

Acknowledgements

My thanks to Liza Fior and Jenny Kingston from muf Architecture/Art and Ken Rorrison and William Owen from London Borough of Hackney for their time and input in meeting me at Kings Crescent, answering my questions, and providing material.

References

Bagnall, A. M., Southby, K., Jones, R., Pennington, A., South, J., & Corcoran, R. (2023). *Systematic review of community infrastructure (place and space) to boost social relations and community wellbeing: Five year refresh*. What Works Centre for Wellbeing.

Coleman, J. (1988). Social capital and the creation of human capital. *American Journal of Sociology*, 94, 95–120.

Gemmell, E., Ramsden, R., Brussoni, M., & Brauer, M. (2023). Influence of neighborhood built environments on the outdoor free play of young children: A systematic, mixed-studies review and thematic synthesis. *Journal of Urban Health*, 100(1), 118–150.

Gill, T. (2007). *No fear: Growing up in a risk averse society*. Calouste Gulbenkian Foundation.

Gill, T. (2021). *Urban playground: How child-friendly planning and design can save cities*. RIBA Publications.

Holloway, S. L., & Valentine, G. (2000). Children's geographies and the new social studies of childhood. In S. L. Holloway & G. Valentine (Eds.), *Children's geographies: Playing, living, learning*. Routledge.

Jacobs, J. (1961). *The death and live of great American cities*. Random House.

James, A., Jenks, C., & Prout, A. (1990). *Theorizing childhood*. Polity Press.

Karsten, L. (2011). Children's social capital in the segregated context of Amsterdam: An historical-geographical approach. *Urban Studies*, 48(8), 1651–1666.

Lambert, A., Vlaar, J., Herrington, S., & Brussoni, M. (2019). What is the relationship between the neighbourhood built environment and time spent in outdoor play? A systematic review. *International Journal of Environmental Research and Public Health*, 16, 3840.

London Borough of Hackney. (2021). *Growing up in hackney child friendly places supplementary planning document*. London Borough of Hackney. Retrieved July 23, 2023, from https://hackney.gov.uk/child-friendly-spd

London Borough of Hackney. (n.d.). *The kings crescent story*. Retrieved July 20, 2023, from https://hackney.gov.uk/kings-crescent-estate

Mayor of London. (2012). *Shaping neighbourhoods: Children and young people's play and informal recreation: Supplementary planning guidance*. Mayor of London. Retrieved July 23, 2023, from https://www.london.gov.uk/sites/default/files/osd31_shaping_neighbourhoods_play_and_informal_recreation_spg_high_res_7_0.pdf

Morrow, V. (1999). Conceptualising social capital in relation to the well-being of children and young people: A critical review. *The Sociological Review*, 47(4), 744–765.

Muf Architecture/Art. (n.d.). Retrieved February 14, 2024, from http://muf.co.uk/

Publica & Erect Architecture. (2019). *Making London child-friendly: Designing places and streets for children and young people*. Mayor of London. Retrieved July 23, 2023, from https://publica.co.uk/projects-making-london-child-friendly/

Putnam, R. (2000). *Bowling Alone: The collapse and revival of American community*. Simon & Schuster.

UN Committee on the Rights of the Child (UNCRC). (2013). *General comment 17 on the right of the child to rest, leisure, play, recreational activities, cultural life and the arts (art. 31)*, CRC/C/GC/17. Retrieved July 23, 2023, from https://www.refworld.org/docid/51ef9bcc4.html

Visser, K., & van Aalst, I. (2022). Neighbourhood factors in children's outdoor play: A systematic literature review. *Tijdschrift voor economische en sociale geografie, 113*, 80–95.

Weller, S., & Bruegel, I. (2009). Children's place in the development of neighbourhood social capital. *Urban Studies, 46*(3), 629–643.

10

SHARING THE STREET AND TOWN IS ESSENTIAL FOR CHILDREN'S GROWTH

From the perspective of *machi hoiku* ('community-embedded nursery')

Norie Miwa

1. Introduction: what is *machi hoiku*?

My speciality is in the fields of construction/urban planning, community building, and environmental psychology, and I have researched the relationships between children of different developmental stages, namely, infant and toddler years, school years, and youth, and the community.

In particular, since around 2007, I have been engaged with research and practice focusing on the interactions among infants and toddlers, the places they congregate, and their communities in Japanese cities. There are many nursery facilities in Japan, particularly in urban areas, which do not have nursery grounds or have only very small ones. Many adults pity the children in these facilities for their impoverished environment. Against this background, a representative in Yokohama-shi, Kanagawa Prefecture, speaking for the development of pre-school age children, told me that nurseries make good use of tools such as walk maps to record and capture local resources such as parks in the neighbourhood and places children like in the provision of everyday nursery care. The area captured by a single walk map is not large, but the maps allow nurseries to make extensive and in-depth use of various local resources on a daily basis. However, I have found that many nursery leaders are not aware of the need to connect to the communities around their schools and do not know how to build relationships with their communities.

From FY2012, I have been engaged with various attempts to strengthen the tie between the nursery and the community with infants and toddlers at the centre at machi hoiku workshops. Working with two nurseries in Yokohama-shi, I walked repeatedly throughout a small area of the neighbourhood where the children took their daily walks based on different themes.

I defined *machi hoiku* ('community-embedded nursery') in a monograph, *Promoting Machi Hoiku* that summarises the development of my research and knowledge gained from practice:

The aim of 'machi hoiku' is to enrich children's lives further. It does not only refer to activities outside the nursery or educational facilities. I define 'machi hoiku' as making good use of various resources in the community for nursery care, expanding the relationship by connecting encounters in the community, and working with the local community to prepare the ground for children to grow in the community by not enclosing children but opening up venues and opportunities.

(Miwa & Ogi, 2017)

2. The group and mimicry that are essential for children's development and the community that provides them

Human beings cannot biologically raise their children without being in a group, as discussed in Chapter 2. Both children and parents grow in naturally formed groups with other parents and children, siblings with children, and so on and by mimicking child-rearing.

However, the past large family and group child-rearing styles that once were common have undergone major changes in modern society due to changes in the family form. Specifically, because of the rise of the nuclear family, the opportunities for multiple adults to be involved in child-rearing have decreased dramatically, and it is now common for both parents to work. This has imposed some restrictions on child-rearing within the family and caused changes in the division of labour. We can no longer expect environments in which family members congregate and imitate one another.

Until a few decades ago, it was taken for granted that adults in the community who were not parents would reprimand children they saw engaging in dangerous activities, watch over them, and protect them; this also supported the children's development (Omameuda et al., 2023). However, since communities have changed, this can no longer be expected. In contemporary society, where the nuclear family is dominant and the number of children continues to decline, I believe that we have reached the stage when society as a whole needs to be acutely aware of how to facilitate child-rearing in a group in a contemporary manner. Child-rearing can no longer be contained in the family, the private sphere, but has to be proactively carried out in the public sphere.

At nurseries, kindergartens, and childcare support facilities where children congregate, there are naturally occurring groups and mimicry. However, if the facilities are closed to the world and staffed by a particular kind of people only, there is no diversity in the groups or the mimicry. When I researched nursery facilities in Yokohama-shi, I observed the facility 'receiving/accepting the community' through volunteering or an open nursery ground scheme and the facility 'going out to the community' by interacting with old people's homes and schools. There was also a nursery located at the corner of the local high street because there was an adventure park or promenade in the neighbourhood. Another facility had a cafe on its premises and the other opened its grounds to the neighbourhood as a promenade. I believe all these instances represent event-making to produce relationships with others by sharing the street and community, which is essential for children's development. It is a strategic mindset to welcome others and utilises the community to realise diverse groups and mimicry.

3. Walking the street from the children's perspective

Another point I have focused on to express using the community to realise groups and mimicry is the culture of walks at Japanese nurseries, which share the streets and prepare walk maps. Here, the daily outing from the nursery was not simple travel to a destination. Rather, 'walks' constitute a culture, and that culture is embodied in the medium of the 'walk map'.

Walk maps are maps that parents develop by mapping different destinations and routes in their neighbourhoods so that children can safely and securely be raised in the community. Nursery teachers take the maps out into the community with their wards to develop the maps. I came up with an idea to revise the children's walk maps by using the nursery as the base and walking around the community with them, checking and testing various resources with parents and a diverse range of local people who do not have close contact with nurseries. The information I collected was shared.

The community is full of different people, things, places, and events. Many of the walk maps I collected contained detailed information such as 'This park has pretty flowers', 'The park has a lot of space and is ideal for hide-and-seek', 'You can find many acorns in autumn in this park', 'A good view of the conductor from this land bridge', 'This bakery is where the nursery purchases its bread', and 'The trees at the corner of the street have a lot of nuts/fruits in autumn'. We can easily picture children enjoying the scenery using their five senses during their daily walk.

Following this, the machi hoiku workshop started with the idea that adults walk around slowly observing the environment from the children's perspective and that when they find anything that captures their attention, they stop and take a photo or record their observations to review the walking routes. For infants and toddlers, we hosted the kids cameraman workshop (Figures 10.1 and 10.2).

In the workshop, when children found anything fun or that caught their attention, they were asked to take a polaroid photo of the object. We then displayed in the nursery what they found, where it was found, and what they

Sharing the street and town is essential for children's growth 149

FIGURE 10.1   A girl takes a picture of flowers in her garden at the kids cameraman workshop.

FIGURE 10.2   A boy takes a picture of an ornament on the front porch at the kids cameraman workshop.

FIGURE 10.3   A man receives a thank-you card and an explanation from the children.

said when they found it to show to their parents when they came to collect their children. The children were proud to show off their photos to their parents.

In the second year of my activity, there was a machi hoiku workshop in which I felt strongly felt that the community had accepted the nursery staff; it was a turning point. It was called 'the big operation THANK YOU'. We made thank-you cards with photos of various items lining the street, such as flowers grown in the garden, nuts and fruits the children enjoyed looking at, figurines of well-known characters children liked, items the children saw and enjoyed during their daily walk, and words of gratitude. The event was to walk around while delivering these cards. Both nursery staff and children were anxious about how they would be received when knocking on doors, but everyone received the card gladly, even if they were a little surprised and shy (Figure 10.3).

Looking after one's front yard and placing objects in the garden is a private activity that families carry out for their own enjoyment. No residents were displeased, however, when they realised that their private activity was providing pleasure and enjoyment to strangers. After that, some families started to deliver vegetables grown in the garden allotment, and some would exchange greetings with nursery staff on their way to or from work. The relationships between the two started to deepen on a daily basis.

4. Connection and participation through the machi hoiku workshop

In Japan, we often encounter a 'safe and secure map' or 'playground map' made by the local residents' association and primary schools. The walk map produced by the nursery also captures local resources, and the process of sharing these resources through the machi hoiku workshop has provided an opportunity for the two parties to connect. When this works well, it leads to new discoveries of the community's attractions, which fosters new relationships between the two. To address the challenges many nurseries face, such as not knowing how to build relationships with the community while being aware of the need to connect with their localities, it was important to think about the design for participation. For this reason, I was mindful that my activity should be an extension of daily nursery activities, that parents should be able to keep up with their motivation, and that events should not be large in scale or about repairing the facility; thus, they could be facilitated reasonably easily.

By inviting the people I met through the machi hoiku workshop to join the daily walk or by accepting them as nursery volunteers, the nursery got to know many residents and the community accepted the nursery as 'a resident', which facilitated a relationship that is conducive to collaboration and co-operation.

5. The ripple effects in the community induced by the machi hoiku workshop

As I conducted the machi hoiku workshops, I began to feel ripple effects in the form of improved relationships between the children and community with the infants and toddlers at its axis so that they grow together. The big operation THANK YOU led to a touching incident.

By the wall near the front porch of a house, a few steps up, was a stone statue of Totoro. However, as children are short, during their daily walk they could only see Totoro's back from the street. Still, the children knew it was Totoro because of its silhouette, and they named that house 'Totoro's house'. It became one of the landmarks on their daily walk. Through the workshop to deliver the thank-you cards, the owner of the house learned that the children were looking forward to seeing the back of Totoro, and when we delivered the card, he was so moved that he opened the gate and welcomed the children in. The children, who for the first time got to see Totoro from the front, were very happy, and the owner looked very pleased (Figure 10.4).

FIGURE 10.4   A girl is happy to meet Totoro from the front for the first time.

A few days later, Totoro was facing the street: the owner had opened his small private space from the gate to the front porch to the public.

By visualising and communicating children's small daily activities through these nursery walks, both the nursery and community started to understand that the two entities were viewing their neighbourhood from very different perspectives. Recognising this facilitated collaboration in improving the neighbourhood's attractions and solving local issues. Through these activities, the community got to know the nursery and accept it as a resident, and the nursery took root and bore the fruits of change in the community. In another instance, infants and toddlers only spend approximately thirty minutes to an hour on their walks, and this covers a really small area, but in that small area, the community and neighbourhood as a whole started to recognise the small children as 'natural' around the community, which was another change.

6. Four stages in machi hoiku: raising children in the community develops the community

So far, I have reviewed the practice of machi hoiku in which children attending a nursery take regular walks in a small area of their neighbourhood based on different themes, visualise the routes on the map, and share it with the local community. There are four stages in this nursery–community relationship: bringing up children connecting with the local community environment, growing up with active participation in the community, ensuring and promoting child development and self-reliance, and developing a child-friendly city as a resilient city for all.

Children went out into the community every day, and although the range of activity was limited, they found and discovered various local resources, exchanged greetings with various people in the neighbourhood, and grew up as the community's children ('bringing up children connecting with the local community environment'). Consequently, children started to grow up with the community as their backyard, became familiar with the neighbourhood, found places they liked, and interacted with adults who they could trust ('growing up with active participation in the community').

From the children's repeatedly walking in the same small area of the community with different perspectives, various neighbourhood organisations and activities became connected, and this resulted in a positive chain reaction as the activities became visible through the media. As the number of opportunities for residents to encounter (find) children increased, the quality of the interactions improved. As a result, the children stopped being 'children from a nursery' but 'children of XX nursery', and the residents started to pay attention to the growth and safety of the 'community's children' who were not their own children or relatives. As more people became involved by greeting and watching over the children, the residents matured to prepare the ground for 'the community itself raising children' ('ensuring and promoting child development and self-reliance').

Furthermore, these activities led to a change in which the nursery felt safer by getting to know many of the people who lived in the neighbourhood and working together with others. Moreover, the activities of the community to develop the children have arguably led to a community where adults and children live together while acknowledging each other and where the community develops resilience against crime and disaster ('developing a child-friendly city as a resilient city for all'). In this way, the practice of machi hoiku has led to the further growth of the community by involving parents and residents and by developing an awareness that the community as a whole raises its children.

7. Capturing the community in which children grow and change in the living sphere

The mobility of infants and toddlers changes by the month, from lying down as newborns (zero years old) to running around at three years old. Consequently, parents' and children's home ranges change.

In my research in Mitaka-shi, Tokyo, and Yokohama-shi, Kanagawa Prefecture, I found that compared with infancy when the majority of parents and children visit commercial facilities, the most common destination for toddlers with a developing sense of self is a park in the neighbourhood (children's or community parks) primarily due to the physical proximity. The average amount of time taken to get to the park was between 5 and 8 minutes, which roughly corresponds to 300–500m when walking slowly at 60 m/minute. This figure suggests a very limited range of mobility, which demonstrates the difficulty for the adult in moving with crawling or running children while paying full attention to them. However, in my view, this range represents a specific and smallest 'local community' in which infants and toddlers grow. In other words, for infants and toddlers, the range of their daily life ('infant's living sphere') is not too big, and in my view, represents the smallest range for child-rearing in groups in contemporary society. The area covered by the nursery's walk, which I have been examining, is about this size (Miwa, 2023a).

In Japan, children start to walk on their own when they start primary school. Their daily living sphere (typically) expands to the primary school catchment range (generally around a 500 m radius), the expansion of their home range and the challenge of walking alone are important milestones in children's growth. At the same time, it is not difficult to imagine that for children to take on that first challenge without fear or hesitation, it would help enormously if they and their parents knew this tiny range of 300–500 m very well from infancy. I believe that for contemporary child-rearing in groups, a well-developed urban environment is necessary for children's development beginning in the infant's living sphere, and it is necessary to make full use of it by understanding it well. Furthermore, it is important to develop an awareness that the small-range local community is in fact the major actor in raising children.

Research on mothers with a first newborn before and after giving birth and their interactions with their communities shows that even mothers who used to frequent a variety of places before giving birth find that their visits become homogenised after giving birth, and they visit considerably fewer places; however active new mothers used to be, after giving birth, their home ranges shrink. Thus, based on the assumption that after giving birth, the mother's opportunities to go out will be dramatically reduced and their home range will shrink, it is important to understand the infant's living sphere before giving birth. That is, during pregnancy or even before, women could begin anticipating the upcoming changes in their living spheres by forming relationships with the community from an early stage, using the local resources in their infants' living spheres, which are smaller than the primary school catchment area, to prevent anxieties about child-rearing and to contribute to realising contemporary child-rearing in groups.

Researchers have found that people with acquaintances in the neighbourhood and with many places to visit are more likely to want to settle. To reduce the diverse worries of the childcare generation and to contribute to

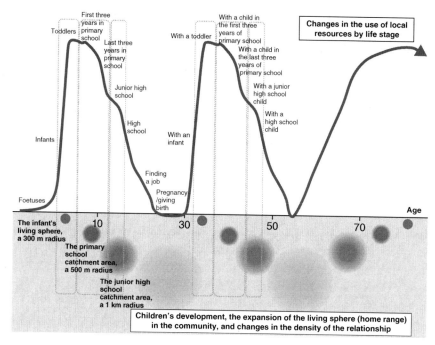

FIGURE 10.5 The expansion of the living sphere in Japan and changes in the relationship with the community by life stage.

children's healthy development, it is essential to increase the number of people who are sympathetic about child-rearing and the number of places to visit in the neighbourhood within a small-range community (Figure 10.5).

8. Building a mutually supportive relationship based on living sphere by life stage

We often encounter the phrase '(to) develop children in the community' in white papers, policies, and plans relating to children or childcare in Japan. The community carries a heavy expectation to develop sociability in children in the role of being the 'public' due to the decline in the number of children and the spread of the nuclear family. However, while in the past, a personal relationship that supports a child's development could have been formed without any intervention, in contemporary society, it needs to be built consciously and strategically. In 'bringing up children in the community' in particular, adults who are not raising children or who do not have opportunities to interact with children might not clearly understand that they have that role or to what if any extent they should be involved.

Figure 10.5 shows the axis of life stages. From a bird's-eye view, the figure shows that the living sphere shrinks in size a total of three times during one's life: as children, as parents adjusting to life with children, and in old age when physical abilities decline; from the community's perspective, these three generations share the community as the infant's living sphere. In other words, we can picture the infant's living sphere not as the relationship of 'giving–receiving' childcare support but as a 'mutually supportive living sphere' where residents of the small-range community are the main actors in child-rearing in groups. The machi hoiku perspective tells us that to develop children in the community, it is necessary to start with being interested in and paying attention to the 'community's' children in your living sphere (Miwa, 2023b).

9. Conclusion

The nursery involved in the machi hoiku workshop discovered many spots that the children liked while taking their daily walk in the neighbourhood; when we connected these spots, a number of fun walk routes resulted. There was a route to look for colours in the community such as red or blue, one to look for trees with flowers and fruits, and one to look for objects that look like a face. At the beginning of the 'Walk Handbook', compiled to be distributed to residents and parents, the nursery head contributed the following:

> The Walk Handbook is produced by our children. Over the past five years, they have taken a walk in the community and each one of them took a photo of a place they liked. We are very encouraged when community members speak to us when we are on our walk. I would be most pleased if some families start taking a walk in the community on their days off with this handbook and if they are excited at the prospect of making new discoveries.

The message contains, along with gratitude for making use of the community, an expectation that parents will become more caring towards the community in which 'others' meet and watch over their children. Compared with their parents, who are not in the community during the day, the children who take a daily walk in the community are experts on the community. The community itself is utilised in the children's development. Therefore, it is important to create the community's future, which will then in turn produce fans of the community.

Machi hoiku is a methodology of community building involving diverse actors that makes use of local resources to share children's development not only among relatives but also among the community. In community building, a device to afford a sense of ownership and agency to the local community is essential. The perspective of machi hoiku, in which the community is opened for children and children are raised in the community, draws in not only parents and nursery staff who are involved in childcare but also residents to produce an awareness that the community as a whole raises the children. This in turn leads to the further development of the community.

Of late, ideas such as the '15-minute city' or '15-minute neighbourhood' as advocated by the mayor of Paris and Carlos Moreno, proposals for building communities where people can live their lives within walkable range are attracting attention. The small sphere of a 300–500 m radius, the infant's living sphere, and the mutual support living sphere as discussed here correspond to these ideas. I hope many communities in which contemporary child-rearing in groups is possible will be built by strategically promoting participatory and collaborative community building in reference to both hardware and software in this small range backed up by the idea of machi hoiku, which aims to open the community and raise children in the community.

Grant information

This work was supported by JSPS KAKENHI Grant Number JP20H02323.

References

Miwa, N. (2023a). Machi to tomoni kodomo ga sodatu seikatuken. *Japan Association for Real Estate Sciences Academic Journal*, 36(4), 85–89.

Miwa, N. (2023b). Kodomo ga iru machinami. *Ie to Machinami*, 11(88).

Miwa, N., & Ogi, M. (2017). *Machi hoiku no susume (growing up and bringing up in child friendly cities)*. Hobun-sya. ISBN 978-4-89491-332-5.

Omameuda, H., Mitani, D., & Saeki, E. (2023). *Kodomo to shakai – Asobi ga manabi tonaru kodomoshutai no hoikujissenn*. Gakken. ISBN 978-4058019979.

PART V
Conclusion

11
PATTERN LANGUAGES TO RAISE SOCIAL CAPITAL FOR A CHILD-FRIENDLY CITY

Isami Kinoshita and Mitsunari Terada

1. Patterns for rebuilding social capital for raising children

Here, we propose hints for rebuilding social capital for children to play outside and grow up using keywords, illustrations and images, and a few lines of explanation, carefully selected to yield 108 patterns (Kinoshita & Terada, 2023). This is a model for creating social capital related to place based on expanding the scale, such as residences, streets, and housing blocks. It is a design catalogue or design language dictionary modelled after Christopher Alexander's pattern language (Alexander et al., 1977).

These were selected based on the results of a literature search, interviews, questionnaire surveys, and discussions of international joint research. Many examples are mainly based on the assumptions of Japanese society, and items might not apply to other countries overseas owing to cultural differences or missing elements. Therefore, we decided that we could add more items to the 108. The results are measured by the indices of children's outdoor play, the openness of the space, and social capital, and they are listed for a space design that incorporates soft aspects to raise these indicators.

The relationship of pattern language and social capital of child-rearing

Christopher Alexander devised the pattern language because he realised that the quality of space is based on relationships. Good spatial qualities are built on the relationships between places and elements that are often unrecognised and unexpressed. This is an attempt to clarify quality without a name (Alexander, 1979). At first, he applied his background in mathematics, but

DOI: 10.4324/9781003456223-16

when he tried to analyse it with a computer, countless patterns appeared in the output.

A pattern language is similar to the work of a copywriter: naming determines the impact of its signification. However, when we name things with the words we use, they are defined in spaces that already have names. It thus presents a difficult task. Therefore, we have used illustrations were used as complements; we have also added a few lines of text to convey messages.

The origin of this idea can be found in Alexander's early article 'A City Is Not a Tree', in which he mathematically clarified that the urban planning of famous architects is a tree structure that branches from the centre to the periphery and ends (Alexander, 1966/1965). He showed that it is a semi-lattice structure similar to organic networks everywhere in having a centre and periphery. In explaining this structure, he drew a relational diagram of the groups, organisations, communities, and so on to which humans belong. When the group is drawn as a circle, it overlaps in multiple layers, and the centre does not concentrate on one point. If you think about this, it is only natural that each citizen plays a central role and that the groups they belong to overlap, which is how human societies are built. However, the power control of the ruler becomes a system with a tree-like structure. Architects and city planners tend to approach power structures and form impersonal spaces because of tree-structured ways of thinking. In other words, there is a difference between an artificial city created by one person's thinking and a natural city created by each inhabitant. Alexander (1966/1965), whose treatise developed into a severe criticism of the theory that has driven modern city planning, caused ripples not only in the fields of architecture and city planning but also in other fields.

Especially in the world of philosophy, this corresponds to a time when postmodernism became popular with the development of semiotics. Above all, the concept of 'rhizome' proposed by Gilles Deleuze and Felix Guattari in *A Thousand Plateaus* is similar to the semi-lattice structure (Deleuze & Guattari, 1987). However, while *Plateaus* was published in 1980, Alexander's *A City Is Not a Tree* was published in 1966. Deleuze and Guattari criticised metaphysics for adopting a tree model and proposed a nomadic, intricately intertwined rhizome with no centre, beginning, or end. This seems very similar to the semi-lattice structure of Alexander's criticism of modern city planning, and Nakamura described this similarity. Whereas bureaucratic organisations and the military are trees, both rhizomes and semi-lattices can be regarded as reflecting non-bureaucratic organisations (Nakamura,1984).

The structure of parenting social capital is similar to that of a semi-lattice or rhizome. Social capital is a function of the invisible network of human relationships. When viewed from the perspective of each child as the main player, the environment in which the children grow up resembles a structure in which groups of human beings overlap in multiple layers.

Not segregation but connection

Alexander argued that the quality of a good space lies in the relationship between places and things and that these relationships are nameless and therefore difficult to recognise. By giving names to these relationships, he not only encourages a renewed awareness of them but also devises a pattern language as a methodology for designing spaces based on the composition of relationships.

The world has moved in the direction of seeking convenience and efficiency, and of severing and dividing relationships. Weaving a relationship contradicts this trend. However, the environment in which a child grows cannot be measured in terms of speed or efficiency. Within the animal kingdom, humans are social beings living in groups. To fulfil one's life in society, it is preferable to grow up in society from an early age and go through a variety of experiences. Through interactions with the surrounding environment, assimilation and adjustment are repeated, and personal growth is achieved. Therefore, it is necessary to create environments where children can grow by interacting with a wide variety of people and experiencing social relationships.

In Germany, the Basic Act on Youth Development – reflecting the fact that children were involved in the Hitler Youth up to the Second World War – states that it is necessary for children to come into contact with diverse adults and values to grow. It stipulates that various non-profit organisations are involved in raising children and that the government must support them. To this end, various organisations that support children's play have been developed, and partnerships with governments are being promoted. These private organisations collaborate to publish event calendars and guidebooks that centralise information for children. It is also the role of the 'new public' that has replaced the government.

In the future, creating a diverse range of people who will play a role in the growth of children will be an effective policy. Traditional social capital for raising children has the function of socialising children through playing around the streets and meeting and interacting with local people. Children's play on streets, plazas, parks, etc. has decreased, and traditional social capital has declined as people's lives, including those of children, have moved increasingly indoors.

Currently, we are shifting to human networks through IT. However, the need for community action has not disappeared completely. Collaborative efforts by various people are indispensable for developing communities where people can continue to live safely in familiar areas, such as for the growth of children, welfare for the elderly, crime prevention, and disaster prevention. Where traditional communities are declining, these efforts also serve as capacity building for communities by building systems in which traditional community organisations collaborate with volunteer NPOs called theme communities working on specialised issues. (Kinoshita, 2006).

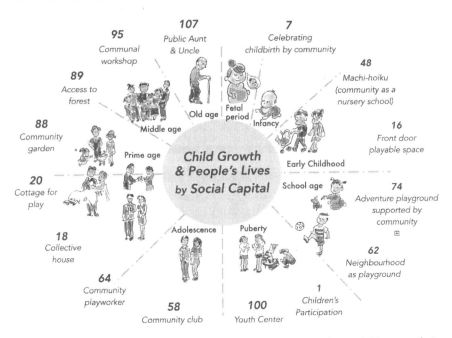

FIGURE 11.1 Some examples of the pattern languages involved in a child's growth & people's lives sustained by social capital.

The social capital of child-rearing is also based on place-dependent traditional concepts, and building links with wide-area networks that spread alongside new modern concepts will help children grow up in contact with the different values of diverse people. This is an important direction for children's growth and socialisation. Various efforts are required to consciously connect children's developmental environments, which will continue to divide various elements if left as it is. And this will create a world that enriches people's lives (Figure 11.1).

2. Pattern languages for child-friendly cities

As one of these efforts, we recommend creating community development plans for raising the social capital that nurtures children's growth by playing outdoors using these pattern languages (Kinoshita & Terada, 2023). We will show the summary of patterns.

How to use a pattern language

A pattern language contains words, illustrations, and commentaries that provide hints for creating a community with rich social capital where children can play and grow outdoors. Figure 11.2 gives an example of how.

Raising social capital for a child-friendly city 165

FIGURE 11.2 A pattern language for a child-friendly city.
Source: Mariia Ermilova ©.

Step 1: read and select

Read the text of patterns of interest from the list or allowing serendipity to guide selection. After surveying the entire book, select the five patterns that seem most significant.

Step 2: look around the town

Using the five selected patterns as a reference, inspect your town and identify any extant patterns. If none exist, remain alert for opportunities to instantiate patterns. Inspection by children and multigenerational groups also enables valuable discoveries. If a more compelling pattern name than the prescribed one emerges, annotate the given name in this text with the preferred nomenclature.

Step 3: develop a strategy for actualising a pattern

Consider the strategic narrative by conferring with children, multigenerational residents including child-rearing households, and professionals from diverse domains about required actions for actualising this pattern. Refer to other pattern cards to inform connections, priorities, procedures, and scenario building. Evaluate relevance and synthesise an integrated plan for your city.

Step 4: attempt feasible actions

Then, undertake activities to recreate the pattern. As time is collaboratively spent on these activities, residents will increasingly contemplate the landscape where children are reared, thereby actually shaping the geography through the pattern and ultimately cultivating community development. Rather than seeking complete instantiation, just make progress to the extent possible. Flexibility and ongoing modification guided by practical experience are advised.

The pattern language

A list of patterns is shown in Table 11.1. We then select 50 patterns related to the matters covered in this book and introduce them with illustrations. Only the title and summary of the remaining patterns will be displayed.

TABLE 11.1 Pattern Language Patterns for Child-Friendly Cities (Kinoshita & Terada, 2023) *(Numbers in grey boxes have a corresponding illustration.)*

No.	Name of pattern	No.	Name of pattern
1	Children's participation	18	Collective house
2	Life stage and living area	19	Cooperative house
3	Child development and housing	20	Cottage for play
4	Childhood's domain	21	Eco-village
5	From screen time to green	22	Housing complex with vegetable garden
6	A safe and secure environment where adults can see	23	It takes a village to raise a child: social care
7	Celebrating childbirth by community	24	Children's emergency shelter
8	Child friendly housing development	25	Renovating empty house
9	Children's room	26	Housing complex revitalisation for multiple generations
10	Family gathering space	27	Common for 8 households
11	Kitchen cooking with children	28	Relatives living nearby
12	*Engawa*	29	Working place nearby home
13	Common lobby	30	Affordable housing
14	Houses with green roofs	31	Neighbours' children can be entrusted
15	Open garden	32	Neighbourhood as a priority for living
16	Front door playable space	33	Street pattern
17	Semi-public space	34	Traffic calming: streets children can play

(Continued)

TABLE 11.1 (Continued)

No.	Name of pattern	No.	Name of pattern
35	Child-friendly traffic rules	73	Under elevated tracks
36	Play street	74	Adventure playground
37	Pedestrian deck connecting play spaces	75	Gathering around fire
38	Green way	76	Playground rules
39	Footpath in the farmland	77	Playbox
40	Cat walkway	78	Small neighbourhood parks
41	Street guarded by Jizo		
42	Place to sit for a few minutes	79	Pocket park
43	Community notification board	80	Festival square
44	Strolling and loitering	81	Open shrine precincts
45	Walking network	82	Scary place
46	Front shop school	83	Place of exploration
47	The street is a stage, the city is a theatre	84	Grass field
48	Machi hoiku (community as a nursery school)	85	Climbable tree
49	Playful kindergarten yard	86	Community farm
50	Nature nursery	87	Edible landscape
51	Town as a school	88	Community garden
52	Green schoolyard	89	Accessible *satoyama*
53	Playable biotope	90	Secret base
54	Open schoolyard	91	Liveable waterfront
55	School farm	92	Under the bridge
56	School social worker	93	*Tamariba* (hangout)
57	A place just to be	94	Mom-and-pop candy store
58	Community club	95	Communal workshop
59	After-school café	96	Children's dining
60	Consolidated school buildings	97	Children's cafés everywhere
61	Empty classrooms	98	Small tutoring school
62	A whole town as a playground	99	Children's play centre
63	Committee for Children's Play	100	Youth centre
64	Community playworker	101	Neighbourhood house for 0 to 100 years old
65	Mobile play		
66	Hospital play	102	Local children's club
67	Child-rearing support after disaster	103	Communal events as rites of passage
68	Playground for disasters and emergencies	104	Immigration, child-rearing, and town upbringing
69	The children's city	105	Roadside station
70	A park created by children	106	Familiar care coordinator
71	Inclusive playground	107	Public granny and grandpa
72	Skateboard park	108	Your pattern

(*Continued*)

TABLE 11.1 (Continued)

1. Children's participation	5. From screen to green
Children have the right to participate in society from their birth.	Induce play that connects the play on-screen to real outdoor play
Children are protected and cared for, but they must be guaranteed the ability to express their opinions and participate in matters related to themselves as subjects no different from adults. This is the basic principle that leads to a sustainable future. The places where children's participation is guaranteed are also social capital, leading to the development of communities in which people can continue to live.	Places must allow for creating rich outdoor play spaces that expand from screens (online games, etc.) to outdoor play in green spaces (outdoors) and allow free interaction with those spaces.

6. A safe and secure environment where adults can see	8. Child-friendly housing development
Children play freely, and adults pay attention when something goes wrong.	Building a living environment that supports the growth of children
To guarantee children's freedom to play outdoors, it is desirable to have a system that allows adults to enjoy their lives outdoors as much as possible; quickly sense crises such as crimes, accidents, and disasters; and deal with them as soon as possible.	Sustainable housing development requires not only infrastructure development but also the added value of creating a framework for building social capital. We look forward to the promotion of residential area management through public–private partnerships by various entities.

(Continued)

TABLE 11.1 (Continued)

12. *Engawa*

Contact point connecting inside and outside

An engawa is a porch connecting the inside and outside of the house and a place to connect people and generations. In Japanese houses, such as farmhouses – which is an intermediate space between the outside and the inside, connects people inside and outside the house. Activities to create new places for interaction, such as community engawa, are also emerging.

16. Front door playable space

2 m setback play space

If the streetside areas become richer, children, adults, and outdoor life will also become richer. Buildings set back from the roadside can support public open spaces, and overall, the social capital of the neighbourhood will increase.

17. Semi-public spaces

The charm of the fusion of public and private spaces

When the boundary between private land and public space on the site is richly connected as a quasi-public space, movement becomes fun, and continuity is created in the cityscape.

18. Collective houses

Living with collaborative housework

If you raise children only in a dual-income nuclear family, you will not have any leeway in your daily life. Living in a collective house where household work is performed collaboratively gives adults a sense of leeway, and children interact with adults who expose them to diverse ideas. A wide range of life experiences gives meaning to growth.

(Continued)

TABLE 11.1 (Continued)

19. Cooperative house

20. Cottage for play

Living together to build social capital for raising children

A base for adults and children to regain their playfulness in nature

People who are thinking about their own housing get together in a 'touch this finger' style and participate in the planning stage to create collective housing. It is expected to spread widely as a collective housing construction where human relationships between residents are built through the construction process and social capital for raising children is formed.

For adults, the activity of living in nature away from their usual work and life is recreation that refreshes one's mind and body. Children are also inspired by adults having fun playing with their own ingenuity and concentration, playing with nature, and learning how to live.

23. It takes a village to raise a child: social care

32. Neighbourhood as a priority for living

Social care is not influenced by the environment of birth.

Housing meets the needs of families raising children.

Alternative nurturing settings, such as orphanages and home-based social care, are shifting to smaller-scale home- and village-based warm environments. To ensure that this does not impede their lives or future career choices, they should be guaranteed a life in which they can form relationships with a diverse range of people.

It is important to choose a house that realises the lifestyle desired by the family. It is desirable for children to be provided with a living environment in which they can grow through a variety of life experiences and to be able to choose.

(Continued)

TABLE 11.1 (Continued)

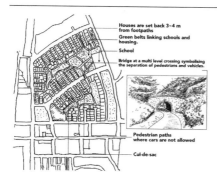 

33. Street pattern

Street network to control car intrusion and speed

The concept of a street network that separates pedestrians and vehicles in suburban residential developments has been applied to existing residential areas. Ingenuity in traffic regulations and road structures will allow children to play and community life to coexist with cars in residential areas.

34. Traffic calming: Streets children can play in

Making the community street in front of the house a place for children to play

Traffic calming restores human life to streets in residential areas occupied by cars. It is necessary to revise traffic laws to allow streets to be used as places for children and adults to enjoy outdoor activities, such as children's play or long tables.

36. Play street

Temporarily turn streets into playgrounds with time restrictions

Reassessing opening playground streets as means of building social capital along street sides and promoting doing so as a new measure rather than a temporary measure will prevent children's solitary deaths and social withdrawal, and enhance disaster and crime prevention.

38. Greenways

Green network axis

The effective placement of greenways will create safe commuting routes that connect parks and schools, a network of playgrounds, and walking paths for people of all ages; provide chances for meeting people; encourage conversations on the streets; and allow children to meet and interact with various people. Greenways are effective for building social capital.

(Continued)

TABLE 11.1 (Continued)

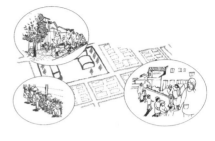

44. Strolling and loitering

Nature by the roadside

The sounds of leaves rustling against each other, small insects, seasonal changes in the colours of plants and sunlight, the smell of the wind, and other discoveries on the roadside are unique to walking. In such a daily life, I want to cherish the time and feelings of admiring the greenery.

45. Walking network

A walking route that enriches moving

Instead of travelling with the goal of heading somewhere, 'walking' is a way to repeatedly enjoy a small, narrow area with different themes. A network route that connects local resources, such as parks for children in a narrow living area that serve as a base for activities, should be a route that can be fully enjoyed in itself rather than simply a travel route to the park.

46. Shopfront school

Work and activity in the town

Education is not something that only schools are responsible for. Children grow up receiving nutrition from the land and the environment, where they grow up and gain wisdom from the activities of the local people. Therefore, it is desirable for children to participate in these activities.

48. Machi hoiku (community as a nursery school)

Raise children in the town, grow the town

By raising children in the town through daily walks and greetings, the children will eventually become independent and grow up in the town. The town raises the children, and the town grows through the children.

(Continued)

TABLE 11.1 (Continued)

49. Kindergarten yard and playground

The garden is a place where children nurture the power to live.

The gardens of kindergartens and nursery schools are not just for the annual sports day; they are places for the daily growth of children. Children's zest for life is nurtured from the creation of a garden rich in nature that nurtures sensibility. Creating a meaningful garden is the starting point of childcare and education.

50. Nature nursery

Free childcare that nurtures children's independence in nature

The 'forest kindergarten', free childcare where children can play in nature every day, is quietly spreading. Being covered in soil and surrounded by greenery stimulates all five senses and the children's instincts as living beings.

52. Green schoolyard

Changing the schoolyard surface from artificial covering to a natural environment.

It is necessary to change schoolyards from artificial to natural coverings, such as soil, turf, and grassland, or to restore them to the natural environment. This creates an environment where children can grow safely and flexibly through various sports activities.

53. Playable biotope

Children's play is also part of the ecosystem.

When we say biotope, the goal is to preserve the habitat of living things, and children's play tends to be excluded. However, children's play is also a part of the ecosystem, and it is necessary for children to have environments where they can play and experience connection with the ecosystem.

(Continued)

TABLE 11.1 (Continued)

58. Community club

Children, young people, and adults are connected.

As the number of children attending after school clubs has increased, NPOs and other organisations have begun to create places for them. These after-school bases serve as third places for children (after home and school) in communities where university students and teachers in the field gather.

62. A whole town as a playground

The living environment responds to the growth of children and expansion of their home range.

Children expand their territories by walking around their houses, on the road, and with friends as they grow. We should consider how to create cities based on a firm understanding of children's behavioural characteristics.

64. Community playworker

Encouraging community people to support children's outdoor play

To encourage children to play outside while coordinating with community groups and residents, community playworkers provide places for children to play, build connections between people and places that support play activities, and develop the community itself. Community playworkers need to coordinate children's freedom to play outdoors.

65. Mobile play

If play workers and play tools come, it will be an adventure playground.

Outreach activities, where play workers come in play buses, play cars, etc. along with equipment to create places like sudden adventure playgrounds, are trump cards for revitalising stagnant children's outdoor play. It is hoped that these will be deployed at many play bases, such as adventure playgrounds and children's centres.

(Continued)

TABLE 11.1 (Continued)

68. Disaster and emergency playground

Play for children even in an emergency

During emergencies, adults and children are both traumatised, but children cannot verbalise their shock. It is necessary to build support systems that provides care for children's trauma, including providing for play.

70. A park created by children

Children participate in park planning and design

Although parks have been created through the cooperation of residents, few parks have been created with children's participation in the planning stage. Triggered by the independent park development, a sense of self-efficacy and interest in community development have arisen, leading to the development of the next generation of leaders.

71. Inclusive playground

Playgrounds are inclusive not only because of the equipment but also because of the human relationships

Inclusive playground equipment does not make a park inclusive. The park becomes inclusive only when children with and without disabilities can play together.

74. Adventure playground

One adventure playground per elementary school district

Children play by setting various challenges themselves, such as building a secret base hut with waste materials and junk. Even if they fail, they try again and gain confidence through successful experiences. Today's children need playgrounds where they can play freely.

(*Continued*)

TABLE 11.1 (Continued)

76. Playground rules

Signboard showing the decision process

Children learn from familiar rules of use. There is a need for a forum for democratic discussions of familiar community topics such as park usage rules. It is important to post the process and results on signboards when sharing usage rules with children and adults.

78. Small neighbourhood parks

Managing parks that anyone can enjoy

Small neighbourhood parks are the most familiar and easy to use in daily life. These can be gardens for everyone if they are managed in cooperation with the government by the citizens who use them. Urban parks are public spaces for all and are a common property of the residents. Therefore, it is essential for administrators and citizens to work together to develop and operate parks as places where users can do what they want (parks that do not say no).

79. Pocket park

Pocket parks can be temporary

Because pocket parks are narrow, they are often set up facing the street. Therefore, pocket parks are used to take breaks and meet up, creating encounters and connections between people and enriching the streetscape. It could be useful to consider stopping car traffic on their streets and integrating them as event plazas.

80. Festival square

Versatile festival squares show community vitality

In traditional Japanese communities, starting with festivals, people live solemnly in their daily lives for the sake of the stage, and when it comes time to perform on the stage, the role of the town festival is to give children the excitement of waiting impatiently for such a transition between *hare* and *ke*.

(*Continued*)

TABLE 11.1 (Continued)

81. Open shrine precincts

Let's open the shrine and temple precincts to children.

By opening the precincts of shrines and temples, which used to be children's playable space but now tend to be closed and exclude children's play, they become places where children can experience a sacred and spiritual atmosphere.

84. Grass field

A grassy vacant lot

Convert vacant lands into fields where children can play, even if it is temporary. A free playground like Kenji Miyazawa's Polano Plaza, which you can reach by counting the number of white clovers.

86. Community farm

A place where anyone can be in charge of an animal

Raising livestock and other small animals in the community, such as at City Farms, is of great significance, and not just for school animal keepers. Taking care of animals is a great deal of work but is also rewarding. People cooperate with each other through animals and feel connected to living things and the environment, which is a great source of growth for children.

87. Edible landscape

Instinct for life

The mere presence of edible plants such as fruit in a landscape provides a sense of joy and security. It has been a long time since the persimmon thief disappeared; however, an environment in which the ability to determine what can be eaten is nurtured through play will lead to sustainable community development.

(*Continued*)

TABLE 11.1 (Continued)

88. Community garden

Everyone making a garden in the neighbourhood

Plant vegetables on vacant land with adults and children in the neighbourhood and make it a place to celebrate the harvest. The relationships between generations and neighbours will deepen.

89. Accessible *satoyama*

Depth of space with a sense of security

Satoyama is a woodland area located near a populated area. Forests and woods provide a sense of spatial immersion. A deep space arouses a sense of dread and enhances a sense of adventure and playfulness. It is expected that satoyama will be utilised and managed as common community land.

90. Secret base

Build a secret base in a treehouse

Establishing secret bases requires spaces where children can explore and create while being guided by the space. Adults around them are required to keep safe distances and protect their children's secrets.

91. Liveable waterfront

Experience in a chain of rich ecosystem

The waterfront is a place where children can experience a chain of rich ecosystems while playing in the water. However, riverbanks have often been covered with high embankments and concrete revetments for flood control, and the relationship between the people and the river has become distant. Therefore, it is necessary to develop environments that are compatible with waterfront play, including safety and biodiversity conservation.

(*Continued*)

TABLE 11.1 (Continued)

94. Mom-and-pop candy store

Alternative home place for children

Dagashi shops (mom-and-pop candy stores) are third places for children. Dagashi ('cheap sweets') are attractive to the children, but without trying, the shopkeeper will recognise the children and talk to them. The dagashi serve as bases for socialising children.

95. Communal workshop

Sharing tools and passing on knowledge and skills to generations

These workshops arouse children's curiosity about creation and help them hone their DIY skills even if they do not become craftsmen or creators in the future. They are also places for mutual aid in the community, including for adults, and for forming creative social capital.

99. Children's play centre

Other options for third spaces for children

While there are fewer places for children to deepen their relationships with friends after school, the role of children's centres is increasing. Therefore, it is expected that children will be involved in the planning and operation of such sites, creating child-centred spaces and developmental activities.

100. Youth centre

Institutions for adolescents by adolescents

There are few facilities for young people in Japan, such as youth centres, which are widely used in Western countries. It is necessary to create facilities that emphasise management by young people, and it is essential to assign youth workers who can support young people.

(Continued)

TABLE 11.1 (Continued)

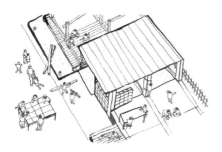 

101. Neighbourhood house for 0 to 100 years old	108. Public granny and grandpa
Supports multigenerational creative activities	Peace of mind for both children and older adults
Rather than separating into children's centres and adult community centres, everyone benefits from intergenerational communication and interaction, such as by teaching and being taught. Opportunities for cross-learning increase, and social capital is built from raising children.	As more and more people live in nuclear families, children's interactions with grandparents and younger generations are limited. Elder volunteers can interact with children in controlled settings with local officials present when it is not possible to casually interact with different generations in the community.

Note: Shaded boxes denote patterns that are illustrated in the table.
Source: All illustrations © Eri Nakada, excluding Figures 12 and 33.

The remaining 58 patterns, without illustrations

2. Life stage and living area

    Relations with the community starting from the living area of infants. It is important to understand children's upbringings and their living spheres, and it is important for people who do not have direct contact with children to keep that in mind and establish a living environment and community development.

3. Housing and children's development

    'Home' brings peace of mind and trust to children's lives.

    Home consists of a house and garden. If home is a place where children can spend time with peace of mind, they can build relationships of trust based on their life experiences.

4. Childhood domains

    Stimulus and response and stimulus and . . .

    Children grow through interactions with their surrounding environment. At each stage of development, children respond proactively to environmental stimuli prompted by intrinsic motives.

7. Community celebrates childbirth

   Connecting the celebration of the birth and the appreciation of the welcome

   The historical ritual of the whole town celebrating children's entrances into this world is still alive, but it is gradually disappearing. I would like to consider a mechanism to bring back the culture of celebrating births with the whole community.

9. Child's room

   Shall we make a child's room, or . . .?

   It is important for children to spend time with their families when they are small, and safe places are necessary for their growth. However, as children grow up, it becomes necessary to consider their privacy; therefore, it will be beneficial for spaces to be flexible.

10. Family gathering space

    Learning how to live and grow

    As members of the family, it is important for children's growth to learn and know the life of the family. Family common space provides opportunities to learn social skills and how to live life while spending time with the family.

11. Kitchen cooking with children

    The first step of participation in housework

    A living space suitable for a child's developmental stage enriches the child's experience and provides food for their growth. It begins with building relationships of trust with the family and the people who live with them, and exchanges with others expand that experience. In other words, family life is carried out according to the child's stage of development, and children learn that they are members of the family by taking on the responsibility of housework. Cooking is the first step.

13. Common lobby

    A place to create opportunities for interaction

    Among the common spaces of residential complexes, the entrance and lobby are the 'nodes' of the buildings. Everyone must pass the mailboxes through the entrance halls to leave these buildings.

14. Houses with green roofs

    Accessibility and ease of use come first

    Rooftop greening has been promoted to mitigate the heat island effect, reduce greenhouse gas emissions, and contribute to the biodiversity of ecosystems. In the case of large-scale developments, decorative rooftop greening can provide accessible and safe playgrounds.

15. Open garden

    Open private gardens to neighbourhood children and families.

    Rather than enclosing the garden with a fence, making it look open to the surroundings not only enhances the green landscape but also serves

as social capital that enriches children's sensibilities, including communication with neighbours.
21. Eco-village
    The chicken is a symbol of circulation and rich social capital.
    Being able to raise chickens is also a symbol of good neighbourhood relationships, and giving children the responsibility of getting the eggs in the morning teaches them a sense of responsibility for and involvement in their community. If you can share and enrich the dining table, your child will also have an experience that is close to that of the ideal farm life.
22. Housing complex with vegetable garden
    Unclear border area coexisting with farming
    In addition to not being surrounded by a fence, the space between the common field and the street, where the border is unclear, becomes a semi-public space for a community with the common goal of growing vegetables, creating an environment in which it is easy to interact with others.
24. Children's emergency shelter
    Child Emergency Shelter stickers, 'Kodomo 110 no Ie', help build social capital.
    "Kodomo 110 no Ie" house stickers are pasted on cooperating houses and stores, mainly on children's school routes. They can be used to strengthen neighbourhood relationships with children and can also increase the human connection to safety and vitality.
25. Renovate empty houses
    Create places for children in vacant houses.
    When residents interact with each other, they can live with peace of mind. Vacant lots, houses, and rooms in a community are local resources that foster connections between people in the community, creating places for children to belong and for community activities.
26. Housing complex revitalisation for multiple generations
    Revitalising housing complexes for multigenerational communication and multicultural coexistence based on meeting halls and plazas
    In ageing housing complexes with declining birthrates and ageing populations, the challenge is to revitalise the complexes for new populations by renovating floor plans and even rebuilding some buildings.
27. Common space for eight households
    Shared outdoor spaces build neighbourhood social capital.
    To create a strong community in an eco-village, a commons shared by eight house units is effective. All edible items are planted there and tended, harvested, and eaten together.
28. Relatives living nearby
    Do not limit child-rearing to relatives only

Parenting is shared among relatives while maintaining a distance that keeps the soup warm and maintains a moderately happy relationship. If different generations can share the infrastructure necessary for their respective lives, living close to each other in comfortable relationships will attract attention.

29. Workplace near home

    Coexistence of workplace and family lives

    It is important when raising children to carve out time that children and parents can share. For this reason, it is necessary for the health of societies for companies to ensure that families with children can spend as much time together as they can.

30. Affordable housing

    Choosing housing that is economically viable and affordable

    Cost is one of the primary considerations when choosing a house, both the cost of buying it and the cost of living in the home.

31. Neighbours children can be entrusted

    Create a modern system of mutual aid relationships.

    Relationships of mutual aid, which are born by establishing relationships with neighbours through family support systems, are not just about taking care of children but also about creating relationships in neighbouring communities.

35. Child-friendly traffic rules

    Community streets and school ways should have traffic signs that children can understand.

    It is time to stop prioritising cars and install traffic control measures including signs that are easy for children to understand, such as on roads in residential areas and along school routes.

37. Pedestrian decks connecting play spaces

    Pedestrian decks separated from the road using the undulations of the terrain

    Combining a green pedestrian path and a pedestrian deck in a planned residential area with undulating terrain provides a comfortable walking path. Children can also go to school safely, play around on their way home from school, and become familiar with the local environment.

39. Footpath in the farmland

    A gentle path where the seeds of relationship with nature grow

    A footpath with soft soil and a waterway on one side can be considered a small biotope that enriches the rice paddy ecosystem. In addition, it invites children to enjoy farming, encounter various creatures, marvel at nature, heighten their curiosity, and enjoy endless play.

40. Cat walkway

    Children open their own path where there is no path.

Children in cities develop as play spaces streets with open street curbs, stepping stones, construction sites, fallen trees, block walls, etc. They respond to spaces that evoke a small sense of adventure and challenge.

41. Street guarded by Jizo

    A symbol of the earth spirit that speaks beyond time and space

    Stone Buddha statues and small shrines are often seen at the borders of villages along old highways and at crossroads. They have the meaning of an amulet from the outside and the origin of the place, and like Jizo-san, they were meant to watch over children, and the children liked to play around them. Just like Jizobon, which is common in the Kansai region, we would like to enliven events that can be enjoyed by people of all generations in the neighbourhood.

42. Place to sit for a few minutes

    Public life for children

    From the inside of a house to the outside, our lives are connected to living spaces. A family can spread to anywhere there is a place to sit for a while. Expanded spaces allow people to connect with each other and foster communities.

43. Community notification board

    Communication through analogue bulletin boards

    Build loose child-rearing networks from bulletin boards that create indirect communication; these allow us to know what kinds of people live nearby without talking with them directly.

47. A street is a stage, a city is a theatre.

    Adults are also characters in the stories of children playing in the street.

    Just as street pianos become street play, adults and children can make their own performances in public spaces, expanding their possibilities and enriching outdoor life and children's play.

51. Town as a school

    Learning through the local environment

    Communities and towns have various learning resources. Considering the entire town as a school, children can create opportunities to explore the area and develop relationships with its people and resources by promoting the learning process.

54. Open schoolyard

    From the open schoolyard to the play centre after school

    Schoolyards are becoming places for children to stay after school, and their scopes are expanding not only for after-school childcare but also for children in general. However, where children are spending much time at school, it is necessary to enrich the spaces with the cooperation of experts, such as playworkers and local residents.

55. School farm
    Open-air school district classrooms
    Promoting farm learning activities at the class or grade level on land that can be used in collaboration with the community within the school district means that classrooms are scattered around the community. This creates opportunities for residents to be involved in teaching children how to grow vegetables.
56. Professional support
    Make networks of specialists who work with children
    Build support teams for children comprising school teachers, people in charge of local welfare and administration, social workers, and psychologists. Make sure children know what resources there are and that experts collaborate with each other.
57. A place to just be
    A place that accepts children silently and watches over them
    The number of children who can't find a place to belong at school, at home, or anywhere else will be saved by having many places in the city that silently accept them and watch over them, saying, 'It's okay just to live'.
59. After-school cafe
    Interacting naturally with local people at school
    Cafés within schools where local people can easily come and go contribute to children's development. Ideally, students should be involved in their operation, but in any case, the cooperation of the community is essential.
60. Consolidated school buildings
    Turning an abandoned school into a school for all generations in the region
    Breathe new life into schools that have functioned as bases for local education and create bases for interactions that transcends generations.
61. Empty classrooms
    Open empty classrooms to the community
    Empty classrooms are referred to as 'marginal classrooms' by schools and the Ministry of Education, Culture, Sports, Science and Technology. Vacant areas are opened to the community, and community organisations such as youth centres and local clubs interact, creating and transmitting activities revitalise the school and the community.
63. Committees for children's play
    In order to comprehensively consider children's play in the community, it is necessary to promote community development where people can play with peace of mind while removing anxiety. To that end, fora for discussion are required among concerned parties that include children.

66. Hospital play
    Guaranteed play during medical treatment and hospitalisation
    To maintain children's quality of life while they are being treated in hospitals and other recuperation environments, it is necessary to create spaces where they can play, such as through hospital play and class or childcare settings.
67. Child-rearing support during reconstruction after disaster
    Prompt response through support and the cooperation of various entities
    During disaster recovery, child-rearing support from entities such as volunteer groups, related organisations, and administrative agencies should be swiftly coordinated to enhance support for children.
69. The children's city
    It is play but "genuine" to create a town managed only by children.
    This is one of the ways for today's children to connect with society when their contact with the real world is fading. From the administration to the shops, the town itself is created and operated only by children. From there, children develop interest and skills in the real world, and adults can't but lend a helping hand.
72. Skateboard park
    What it means to build a skateboard park in the city
    The skateboard park is a symbolic place of youth culture, and placing it in the city conveys the message of a city that accepts and supports young people. If young people who are good at skateboarding teach small children and adults who are beginners and create a place where they can play an active role, they will not be left out, and young people will become the cornerstone of regional exchanges.
73. Under elevated tracks
    Under overpasses is not a negative place
    Roads and railway overpasses have a dark and scary image. There are legal restrictions on the installation of buildings, but there are also examples of the effective utilisation of parks and open spaces through community management.
75. Gathering around fire
    Spending time together while manipulating flames
    Instead of chatting while looking at a PC or smartphone, we watch the fire swaying in the furnace together and have a conversation. Children also learn how to handle and enjoy fires, such as starting fires and roasting sweet potatoes. Amid trivial conversations, people's hearts are at ease, and relationships are built.
77. Playbox
    Make the playground one's own
    For children to feel that the playground is their own, it is important to store a variety of playthings there; rather than waiting for someone to bring them play, they can develop independent play.

82. Scary place
   A place to nurture sensitivity and imagination
   There are good and bad things that are scary. While ensuring safety from crime and accidents, preserving spaces with atmosphere that reflect the history and location of the place enriches children's imaginations.
83. Places of exploration
   Towns where children can explore following their animal instincts
   Cats and other animals explore the expanse of their territories. Children explore towns as they grow and incorporate new discoveries into their territories. This is a basic act for children to interact with the town, and I would like towns to be places where they are allowed to explore freely.
85. Climbable tree
   Natural compound playground equipment that trains the mind and body
   A tree that can be climbed is natural compound playground equipment that requires various movement skills and a sense of balance to 'operate'. When they reach the top, children feel a sense of accomplishment, and by looking down on their friends and towns from above, the children's imaginations expand.
92. Under the bridge
   Secret hideaway
   The atmosphere is chaotic, but one can enjoy outdoor play even on rainy days. Try making a hideaway in the gaps between plants or sit down for a while to rehydrate. It tends to have a negative image, but is also an affordance space that accepts children's daily lives.
93. *Tamariba* ('hangout')
   Places outside school socialise children.
   Tamariba/ibasho nurture relationships besides those at home and school and create opportunities for people to open themselves and build ties with society. Whether they be streets, parks, or children's homes, tamariba are playgrounds that depending on the child.
96. Children's dining
   Triggered by food
   It would be nice to have community kitchens and dining rooms where people can spend time together, including children. Preparing and enjoying meals together lightens feelings and creates connections.
97. Children's cafés everywhere
   Many spaces can be comfortable for children, and it is good for children to have options in different forms. Children's cafés can be such places for them.
98. Small tutoring school
   Serving as a place to stay after school
   In many cases in small tutoring schools where children can walk to school on their own, a friend's mother or a neighbour's aunt plays the role of study teacher. In some cases, it is adjacent to the teacher's residence; in others, a room in a house is used as a cram school.

102. Local children's club
     Familiar areas where children grow up
     Children's local societies are mechanisms for raising children in the community; however, participation rates is on the decline. They should be considered opportunities for children to socialise with each other and with various adults in the community, including parents.
103. Communal events as rites of passage
     Socialising children's growth milestones
     In addition to Shichi-go-san, rites of passage for children's milestones are mechanisms for celebrating their growth with their communities and watching over them.
104. Immigration, child-rearing, and town upbringing
     The attractiveness of immigration is the richness of the natural environment and social capital
     It will be revitalising to review the rich natural environment and the richness of human relationships, where children play and grow up in rural areas, and think about how to make use of these in modern ways through the eyes of immigrants and related populations from outside the municipality.
105. Roadside station
     Michi-no-Eki (roadside stations) with multiple functions
     Roadside stations are not only rest facilities during transit. Depending on the region, they function as regional bases for residents' exchanges, lifelines, playgrounds, and learning facilities.
106. Familiar care coordinator
     Gentle expertise in collecting and connecting voices related to local children
     It is expected that voices about children in the community will be collected and supported by the elderly, that they will be connected to support groups involved in the welfare of children in difficult situations, and that voices of children themselves will be collected and connected to the government.
108. Your pattern
     Please find your pattern which creates child-friendly communities.

Grant information

This work was supported by JSPS KAKENHI Grant Number JP20H02323

Acknowledgements

We gratefully acknowledge the invaluable advice from many experts in the creation of these patterns. We also thank Akiko Kubota (Hayashi) of Kajima Institute Publishing Co., Ltd. for his support in compiling this pattern collection.

References

Alexander, C. (1966). A city is not a tree. *Architectural Forum, 122*(1), 58–62. (Original work published 1965, April)

Alexander, C. (1979). *Timeless way of building*. Oxford University Press.

Alexander, C., Ishikawa, S., & Murray, S. (1977). *A pattern language: Towns, buildings, construction*. Oxford University Press.

Deleuze, G., & Guattari, P. F. (1987). *Mille Plateaux–Capitalisme et schizophrénie 2 [A thousand plateaus: Capitalism and schizophrenia]*, B. Massumi (Trans.). (Original work published 1980). University of Minnesota Press

Kinoshita, I. (2006). Local governance and city planning: Neighborhood community and community development association. In M. Takamizawa (Ed.), *Theory of city planning* (pp. 220–243). Gakugei Publishers.

Kinoshita, I., & Terada, M. (2023). *'Kodomo Machizukuri catalogue' (Pattern language for child-friendly-city)*. Kajima Institute Publishing.

Nakamura, Y. (1984). *JutsugoShu (Predicate collection)*. Iwanami Publishers.

INDEX

Page numbers in *italics* indicate a figure and page numbers in **bold** indicate a table on the corresponding page.

15-minute city 157
15-minute neighbourhood 157

Abendroth 48
Ackermannbogen: 68–71; NachbarschaftsBörse 58; Neighborly Help Association 56–58, 65; obstacles to children's play 71–72; play environments for children 58–63; social capital for children 63–68
Adams, Eileen 22
adults 6, 18, 23, 24, 58, 60, 63, 80, 87, 91, 93, 104, 105, 106, 116, 118, 119–125, 129–130, 134, 142, 144, 147, 153, 163, 168, 169, 170, 174
adventure playground 119, **167**, *175*
affordable housing **166**, 183
affordance 5, 6, 9, 12, 23, 87–89, 94, 95, 97–98, 100, 102, 104–105, 107
after-school café **167**, 185
Alexander, Christopher 161–162
apartment building play areas 93

Basic Act on Youth Development 163
birth rates 17, 24–25, 116
Bourdieu, Pierre 19–21
Bowling Alone (Putnam) 18
bridge **167**, 187
Brundtland Report 21–22
Bullerby model: affordances 6, 23, 96–100; concept 87–89, 102, 106; image/heritage 103; independent mobility 6, 23, 87–88, 94, 97–98
Bullerby Village 23, 116, 117–125

calming rooms 118
Catalog of Criteria for Child and Youth Conform Building and Planning 72–75
cats 118
cat walkway **167**, 183–184
celebrating childbirth **166**, 181
chickens 47
child development 6, 48, *51*
Child-Friendly Cities 22
child-friendly housing development **166**, 168
child-friendly traffic rules **167**, 183
childhood's domain **166**, 180
child-led walks 106, *107–108*, 110; *see also* machi hoiku ('community-embedded nursery')
child-rearing 22, 24, 25, 116, 117, 147, 154–155, 156, 157, 164
child-rearing support/disaster **167**, 186
Children of Bullerbyn Village (Lindgren) 23
children's cafés **167**, 187
children's city **167**

children's club **167**, **188**
children's dining **167**, **187**
children's emergency shelter **166**, **182**
children's participation 21–22, 25, 74, 119, **166**, **168**
children's places 87
children's play centre **167**, **179**
children's play on scheme/adult attitudes 140–142
children's rights 25, 73
children's room **166**, **181**
citizen participation 99
City Is Not a Tree, A (Alexander) 162
climbable tree **167**, **187**
cognitive/social development 6
co-housing 80, 82–83
Coleman, James S. 19–21
collective housing 75, 79–84, **166**, **169**
committee for children's play **167**, **185**
common for 8 households **166**, **182**
common lobby **166**, **181**
communal events **167**, **188**
communal workshop **167**, **179**, **187**
community: action 163; activities 65; building 32, *35*, *41*; child participation 21–22; child-rearing support 24; development in outdoor space design 31–53; empowerment 119; engagement 106, 117, 134; fusion of video games and real play 9; gardens 32, 57, 58, 62–63, *62*, 64, 73, 75, **167**, **178**, **187**; indoor space 57, 58, 62; multigenerational house 82; organisations 163; participation 151–157; playworker 123, *124*, *125*; as potential playground, 11; seasonal play 6; social capital 18–19, 21, 63, 75–76, 103–105, 111–112, 164; supportive role of adults 104–105; sustainable 16; temple 39; values 75; walks 148–151
community club **167**, **174**
community farm **167**, **177**
community notification board **167**, **184**
consciousness: child development 48; developmental stages 48; levels 50; phases of child development as four qualities *51*
consolidated school buildings **167**, **185**
Convention on the Rights of the Child 21, 22, 119
cooperation model 55
Cooperative Erlenmatt 48
cooperative housing 75, **166**, **170**

cottage for play **166**, **170**
Courtyard 1 137, *137*
COVID-19 24

daycare centre 52, 58, 59, *59*, 63
Death and Life of Great American Cities, The (Jacobs) 129
declines in outdoor play/social capital 24
Deleuze, Gilles 162
densification 103, 110–111
designated playgrounds 58
Dewey, John 19, 20, 115
diverse terrains 68–70
diversity 74–75
doorstep play space 131–132, 134, 143–144

eco-village **166**, **182**
edible landscape **167**, **177**, **187**
Eigenheimstrasse/Heimatstrasse 43
elderly generation 64, 71
elevated tracks **167**, **186**
empty classrooms **167**, **185**
empty house renovation **166**, **182**
engawa **166**, **169**
England 103
Erlenmatt 44–48
events 47
everyday morality 133, 143
everyman's right 94
exploration place **167**, **187**

familiar care coordinator **167**, **188**
family gathering space **166**, **181**
family structures 77–78, *78*
fences 71
festival square **167**, **176**
fire gathering **167**, **186**
flexibility 74
footpath/farmland **167**, **183**
free/undefined spaces 58, 60–62, 70, *70*, 96–97
Freidorf, Switzerland: context 31; inspiration 31–32; picture report 33–43
Fröbel, F. 32
front door playable space **166**, **169**

Geddes, Patrick 22
Goedhard, G.J.D.C. *38*
grass field **167**, **177**, **187**
green roofs **166**, **181**
green schoolyard **167**, **173**, **184**

green spaces 68, 103, 105, 106
green time 5–12, 24
greenways **167, 171**
Guattari, Felix 162
gymnastics *35*

Habitat 48
HABITAT II 21
Hanifan, L.J. 18–19
Happy Habitat 20
Happy Habitat Revisited 20
Hart, Roger 23
health 73
Hitler Youth 163
hospital play **167, 186**
housing complex revitalisation **166, 182**

Illich, Ivan 11
independent mobility 6, 23, 87–88, 94, 97–98, 99, 102, 104, 105–106, 112–113
indoor community spaces *57*, *58*, *62*
International Co-operative Day *35*

Jacobs, Jane 19–20, 116, 129–131, 143
Jäggi, Bernhard *38*

Kankanmori 81–82, *81*
Karsten, Lia 87
kindergarten yard **167, 173**
KITA 48, *52*
kitchen cooking/children **166, 181**
kitchen gardens *34*, *36*
Kit, Fence, Carpet approach 11
Kyttä, Marketta 23, 87, 89, 90, 98, 102

Lienhard and Gertrud (Pestalozzi) 32
life stage **166, 180**
life stages 155–156, *155*
Lindgren, Astrid 23, 102, 119, 122
liveable waterfront **167, 178, 187**
loitering 129
Longstocking, Pippi 122–123
Loury, Glenn 19
Lynch, Kevyn 21

machi hoiku ('community-embedded nursery'): concept 146–147, 156–157; pattern language pattern **167, 172**; walks 148–157
machi-work 22
Meyer, Hannes *34*, *36*, *37*, *43*
Million Homes Programme 103

Minecraft 9–10
mobile play 25, **167, 174**
mom-and-pop candy store **167, 179, 187**
Moore, Robin C. 21
Moreno, Carlos 157
Munich Model *55*
Murrain Road play street, 134, *136*, *137*, 141
mutual help 58, 65–66

natural rock formation *95*
nature nursery **167, 173**
neighbourhood **166, 170**
neighbourhood house **167, 180**
neighbourhood parks **167**
neighbours' children **166, 183**
Netherlands 23
NPO Law 18
nurseries 56, 59, 82; *see also* machi hoiku ('community-embedded nursery')

open garden **166, 181–182**
open schoolyard **167, 184**
open shrine precincts **167, 177**
open spaces 23, 44, 69, 102, 103, 105, 112, 118
outdoor play: 3D diagram 25; benefits 6; building/restructuring 26; green time 5–12; number of playing days per week/weekday 16, *17*; richness/variability 5–6; screen time 3, 4, 7–9; video games 3–4, 7–8
outdoor play promoter 122, *124*
Outlook Tower 22

parking space *52*
parks: child created 119, **167, 175**; child-friendly environments 103, 104; debt free 32; impact of development projects 110; institutionalized/planned 11; Kit, Fence, Carpet approach 11; mobile play 25; neighbourhood **167, 176**; pocket **167, 176**; reinvention 11–12; skateboard 141, **167, 186**; social capital 112, 163; socialisation 106; updates 11; use by nurseries 146, 148, 154
pattern languages 25, *165*, **166–180**, 180–188
pedestrian deck **167, 183**
Pestalozzi, Heinrich 32, *36*
physical/mental health 6
place just to be **167, 185**

play 5–12, 21–22, 25, 53, 68, 93–96, 141: holistic ecosystem 11–12; unmanaged 11–12; water 67
playable biotope **167**, **173**
playbox **167**, **186**
play equipment 11, 91, 93, 137, 141
playful kindergarten yard **167**
playground map 151
playgrounds: adventure 119, **167**, **175**; all-weather 42; for children/adults 34; communal 34; continuity of space 70; creation 87; demand 11; designated 58, 59–60; different age groups 56; for disasters/emergencies **186**; disasters/emergencies **167**, **174**; diverse 68–71; diverse possibilities 74–75; fitness 61; functions 25, 106; hill 60; holistic ecosystem 11–12; inclusive **167**, **175**; lawn 42; map 118; places for children 87, 91–93; rules **167**, **176**, **186**; safe 53; safe possibilities 73; socialisation 106; town as **167**, **174**
playleader adults 12
play shelters 67
play space 4, 7, 9, 10–12, 23, 58, 63, 64, 66–68, 70, 71, 74, 89, 92–96, 99, 103, 118, 131, 134, 137, 141, 142, 143
play street 11, 134, 141, **167**, **171**
playworker 119–120, 122–124, **167**, **174**
pocket park **167**, **176**
Pokémon 9
Pokémon GO 9
Portmann, A. 21
private yard play area/surroundings. 93, 94, 96
puberty 48–50
public granny/grandpa **167**, **180**
Putnam, Robert D. 18, 115, 130

Rasmussen, Kim 87, 89, 91
relatives living nearby **166**, **182**
resilience 6
rhizome 162
Rio Global Environment Summit 21
roadside station **167**, **188**
Rousseau, J.J. 32

safe and secure environment **166**, **168**
safe and secure map 151
satoyama **167**, **178**, **187**
scary place **167**, **187**
Schlicht, Ekkehart 19

School and Society, The (Dewey) 19
school farm **167**, **185**
school social worker **167**, **185**
Schulthess, Edmund 37, 38
screen-based play cycle 8, 10
screen time 3, 4, 7–9, 7, 24, **166**, **168**
seasonal play 6
secret base **167**, **178**, **187**
security 73
self-esteem 6
semi-lattice 162
semi-public space **166**, **169**
shopfront school **167**, **172**
sidewalks 129, 142
sitting place **167**, **184**
skateboard park 141, **167**, **186**
social capital: 3D diagram 25; building/restructuring 25, 26; child-friendly environments 103–104; of child-rearing 164, *164*; children and 130–132; collective housing 77–84; community 18–19, 21, 63, 75–76, 104, 164; concept 18–20; declines 24; everyday morality 133, 143; importance 116; neighbourhoods with special qualities for 107–109; pattern languages 161–164; play content as 121; play environment as 121; promotion 23–24; redefinition 21; relationships with neighbours as 121; role of physical environments in forming 105; sustainable 50; traditional/modern 19–20, *20*
social care **166**, **170**
social housing 55
socialisation 6, 18, 23, 25, 63, 80, 106, 129–130, 153
social isolation 17
social networks 65–66
social relationships 20–21
sports fields 93
street pattern **166**, **171**
streets: exploding schools 20; guarded/Jizo **167**, **184**; mobile play 25; play 11, 134; as stage/city as theatre **167**, **184**, vitality of 116
streetscape 95
strolling/loitering **167**, **172**
sustainable development 21–23

tamariba (hangout) **167**, **187**
Thousand Plateaus, A (Deleuze & Guattari) 162
Tocqueville, Alexis de 115

tools 11
Town & Country Planning Association 22
town as playground **167, 174**
town as school **167**
traffic calming **166, 171**
traffic-free areas 71, 73, 105
tutoring school **167, 187**

United Nations Committee on the Rights of the Child 131
upbringing **167, 188**
usability 73

vegetable gardens 32, *42*, *47*, 82, **166, 178, 182, 185**
Verein Erlenmatt 48
video games 3–4, 9

walking network **167, 172**
walk maps 146, 151
walks 106, 110, 148–157
Ward, Colin 20, 22

yakamashi/Bullerby Village 116, 117–125
youth centre **167, 179**
YouTube 12

Printed in the United States
by Baker & Taylor Publisher Services